My Autobiography

My Autobiography

A Personal Journey in Life of a Poor African Boy

I Owe My Success to My Mother and My Wife, Maria,
for Making Me the Man I Have Become

Dudley Lameck

To order additional copies of this book, contact:
Xlibris Corporation
1-888-795-4274
www.Xlibris.com
Orders@Xlibris.com
107973

CONTENTS

To my wife, Maria, thanks for the many years of friendship, love, caring, and support. By believing in me and what we could achieve together, you made it possible for us to live a happy life and reach our goals. You have been my closest adviser and a dedicated nurse during times of illness. This book is dedicated to you.

To my mother (may your soul rest in peace), I owe my success in life to you. You worked hard to take care of us when growing up and made getting education a number one priority for your children. You are our hero, and many thanks to you.

To Fred and Winnie, I love you all very much. This book gives you a very good picture about where I came from and how I became the man I am. I hope you will learn a lot about me from my true story. Maybe you will get something from my experiences that will help you in dealing with problems you face in life. My story shows that the type of life you have is a result of decisions you make daily, your relationship with others, your character and behavior, your determination to reach defined goals, and maintaining good moral values. I am wishing all of you and your families the very best in life. And when I am gone, don't cry because you feel sorry for me; I had a good life. Cry if you will miss our good and loving relationship.

To my beloved readers, I want you to understand that my story is not atypical for African children growing up in a poor family. However, for all kids, one thing is undeniably clear-when growing up, life is tough, and future success is unpredictable. Parents' level of education, their financial status, how they value education for their children, children's interest and determination to succeed in school, and availability of other financial support are major factors that would determine the future life of the child. I was very lucky that although our parents only had elementary education and were very poor, they valued education very much, especially our mother, who made every effort so that all her children got education. We were raised by parents that taught us good moral values, high level of discipline, hard work, and respect for others. I remember my mother telling me, "Don't expect an easy life. You have to prepare for a tough life by working very hard in everything you do. Later, you will enjoy the fruits of your hard work." that is the exact message I told my children, and I hope my readers will do the same.

This book is a true story about my life, a personal journey from childhood to retirement. It is full of twists and turns and unpredictable events. I can say without reservation that it has been a remarkable and memorable adventure.

I was raised, like my sibling before me, in a home where respect, discipline, value of education, and hard work were the norm. We were poor but very happy with what our parents could offer the family. Though our parents were small farmers and had only elementary education, they spent the little money they earned for family matters and to pay for our education. Their main goal was to support us through education so that we could have a better life than the one we had. Mother told me one day, "Life is not going to be easy. Work hard in school and in whatever you do. You will later see the rewards of a better life." Those words of wisdom made me realize that my future depended on my effort and commitment in education and working hard. The family would be there for support only. I believed being poor was not an excuse for failure. I pursued my professional education in the area of agriculture, with the goal of gaining modern technology, which would enable me to give good advice to small farmers like my parents. In November of 1968, I graduated with diploma at Morogoro Agricultural College, now Sokoine University.

For a number of years I worked as an agricultural extension officer in the Ministry of Agriculture. My story shows that my first ten years of professional life had a number of twists and turns where my ability to lead was put to the test.

In December 1981, I graduated with double major, BS in plant science and BS in agricultural education at North Carolina A&T State University, Greensboro North Carolina, USA. I continued with full-time studies while working in the Soil Science Lab, and my wife, Maria, worked full-time for supporting me because I did not have a scholarship. In May 1983, I obtained my masters in agricultural education and went back to Tanzania and worked in the Ministry of Agriculture. In May 1991, I joined North Carolina State University in Raleigh, North Carolina, USA. I worked in the biology lab while going to school full-time. As with my masters, I did not have a scholarship. My wife, Maria, worked with two jobs. I had to prepare meals at home and helped Fred and Winnie with their homework. Life was very tough because both of us were very busy. In May 1998, I completed my doctorate in education with the focus in agricultural education and extension.

My story shows that parents have an important role in raising, supporting, and advising their children during the period of growing up. Children should be told about the importance of good education and that they are in control in determining their future. Parents and other people can only help them to achieve their goal.

ACKNOWLEDGMENTS

I would like to acknowledge my dear wife, Maria, and my children, Winnie and Fred, for their love, support, and encouragement without which this project would not have been possible. Maria worked with two, sometimes three, jobs to support the family and my educational endeavors. She deserves all the credit for the financial contribution which made possible for me to graduate without a debt.

A number of professors also deserve to be acknowledged for their role in providing me with not only academic advice but also part-time research opportunities because I had no scholarship. Professor M.R. Ready, my adviser for my master of agricultural education thesis at North Carolina A&T State University, Greensboro, North Carolina, USA. He also offered me a research assistant position in the soil chemistry lab. And Professor Gail Wilkerson and Professor Mike Linker, both of Crop Science Department at North Carolina State University, Raleigh, North Carolina, USA are acknowledged for the assistant research positions they offered me, which helped to cover tuition for my doctor of education program, focusing on the area of agricultural education and extension. Professor Mike Linker was also a member of my dissertation committee, together with Professor Richard T. Liles, Professor John Pettitt, and chairperson Professor David Mustian.

CHAPTER 1

My Childhood

One thing about human life is that we have no control about what type of our parents should be and where we should be born. And when we come to this world, during the early childhood and teenage years, we are at the mercy of those who have the responsibility of raising us. Being born in a well-to-do family and a good neighborhood with good schools and plenty of economic opportunities or in a very poor family with poor schools and limited economic opportunities and a bad neighborhood can be one of the most important factors in the type of life the child will have in his/her adult life. This, unfortunately, is not unique to African countries but is true throughout the world.

I was born in Tanzania (East Africa) on February 13, 1945, in a small village called Katoke, which is close to Bukoba Town at the shore of Lake Victoria. Typical of a big African family, I was the youngest of seven siblings, five boys and two girls. Our dad, the late Lameck Chilewa, was a cook at a missionary center, and our mother grew crops on a small farm and also took care of us. She also made sure that every child started first grade when they were seven years old.

The head of the missionary center was a preacher called Father Ball. He was from England. When I was born, he suggested to my parents I should be called Dudley, a British name. They agreed, and I was baptized with that name. The best part is that he made arrangements at the missionary dairy farm for my mother to get two pints of cow's milk daily for me free of charge. That offer continued for two years. Thinking now how important good nutrition was at infant age, I can say I was very lucky. And I appreciate what Father Ball did to help me and my parents at that critical time of my life.

I know one of my brothers (out of respect, I won't mention his name) would not want me to tell you about the following story. I was told this story by my mother. One day, as was a normal routine, she gave a small bowl of milk to my elder brother who was holding me. After receiving the bowl of milk, he took me to the back of the house. A few minutes later, he went back to the kitchen where our mother was and said, "Thank you very much." She could not believe what she heard him say. She asked him furiously, "You want to tell me you drank the milk I gave you for the baby?" She got an answer she did not expect. My elder brother said, "I thought that milk was for me." That answer invited a question. She asked him, "When was the last time I gave you a bowl of milk?" There was a brief period of silence followed by a polite request for forgiveness. "Mother, I am very sorry, I will never do that again." It's funny that whenever I visit my brother's family, I always have this in my mind. "Oh, bother, what were you thinking!" The lesson here is that siblings should be good, love and help each other in every way, build a strong and close relationship that would last forever. During tough times in life, you need to have someone whom you know will help you no matter what.

One day, my dad told me about an incident that happened at the missionary center. A laundry worker was told by Father Ball to take care of bedbugs. He said, "There is a lot of bedbugs in my bed, make sure you burn the bedsheets today." The laundry worker replied, "Yes, sir, I will burn the bedsheets this afternoon." About 2:00 p.m., Father Ball was in the office, and as he looked outside, he saw the laundryman standing close to a huge fire. As he came out of the office, he shouted, "Hey! What are you burning?" The laundryman replied, "The bedbugs in the bedsheets, sir." Father Ball was so angry. As he came closer to the fire, he said, "I told you to burn the bedbugs by putting the bedsheets in boiling water and not putting the bedsheets on fire!" The laundryman said, "I am very sorry, sir, but when you said I should burn the bedbugs, I thought you meant burning the bedsheets that has bedbugs." The lesson from this true story is that when you are in a foreign country, trying to communicate with the local person through their local language, make sure he/she understands clearly what you mean. One way you can check if the person understood what you said is by asking him/her to relate back to you what you said.

CHAPTER 2

New Life at Kilimatinde

In the late 1940s, my family moved from Bukoba to a small town called Kilimatinde, in Dodoma Region. Let me tell you a little bit about Dodoma Region so that you can get a good picture of the area around Kilimatinde.

Dodoma Region, where Dodoma City is the capital of the country, is in the center of Tanzania. During the colonial era and few a years after independence (December 9, 1961, is Tanzania's independence day) the capital city was Dar es Salaam, which is at the east coast of the country. It was moved to Dodoma for two reasons: (1) for security as Dar es salaam was vulnerable to enemy attack from the ocean, (2) to bring government offices at the center of the country for easy access by the people, and (3) to reduce transportation cost for managing development projects. Dodoma Region has arid climate. The area receives 25 inches (62.5 mm) or less of rainfall a year between late March and May. Therefore, there is usually a long, dry season and frequent food shortages because many areas have no irrigation facilities. The main local tribe is Wagogo. They grow crops such as millet, sorghum, finger-millet, and a variety of corn adapted to arid conditions. During the month of May, the rainy season ends, and a cool, dry season starts. Some farmers grow tomatoes and other type of vegetables in low-lying areas where there is moisture due to a high water table. Farmers living close to a river or water pond keep goats, sheep, or cattle. Believe or not, they grow and produce wine in Dodoma. Dodoma, the capital, is now a big city and continues to expand. My sister Winifrida Chilewa, a retired nurse (ranked third in the family) and my brother Gilbert Chilewa, a civil engineer (ranked fifth in the family) and my niece Mary Masumbigana (a nurse) live in Dodoma City. During my vacation days, I go to visit them in the city.

Kilimatinde, being in the Dodoma Region, has also a very long dry season and very short rainy season. We had a three-acre farm where we grew sorghum, millet, sesame, and corn enough to feed our family, and we sold the surplus. My parents used the little money we got primarily for paying school fees for my brothers and sisters. Therefore, food shortage was not a big problem for us. Except I remember in the early 1950s that there was very little rain, and the result was a great famine throughout the region. We were lucky to have a little bit of food in our storage facility outside our house.

The main tribe at Kilimatinde is Wagogo. The name may sound strange and funny, but they are very friendly and nice people. I have no idea why my parents decided to settle at Kilimatinde, such a dry place with no hope of good life. I wish I could ask my late dad during the living years. This is another good lesson: children should talk to their parents and ask whatever they want to know about the family history while they are still with them. Because once they are gone, the information they did not tell them will be gone forever.

One evening, as we sat eating dinner, one Mgogo (singular of Wagogo) knocked at the door and asked if he could join us at the table. We were not surprised by his request because we knew there were many people who were facing food shortages. But when he wanted to start eating without washing his hands, my dad shouted to him, "Not in this house! You have to wash your hands first before you can sit at the table to eat." He eagerly complied, and as he ate, he started asking a bunch of questions and making jokes. The trick was to make everybody laugh in order to slow down their eating while he ate as fast as he could. Dad noticed what was going on and said, "Hey! This food is for everyone, and it is not running away, slow down." He was very embarrassed when he realized that everyone was staring at him. He knew that his trick had failed. Because of the hospitality he was given, he did not know what to say. You see, sometimes a few words can teach somebody a big lesson. That is one of the things I learned from Dad, that you have to take advantage of a teachable moment.

It was a family tradition to eat together at breakfast, lunch, and dinner for those who were at home. I remember Dad laying out the following table manners: (1) no talking when eating because the mouth should have only one thing to do and that is chew the food thoroughly and (2) eat slowly; there is no reason to eat fast because the food is not running away. That is a tradition I passed on to my children.

In 1949, our last born, Geoffrey, was born. Therefore, in the family ranking, I became the second to our last born. Mom now was very busy taking care of the infant and me and my brother Rhone who now was six years old. He was born 1943. Dad was a businessman and was away from home for many months. His tendency of being away for a long time on business trips continued for many years. Therefore, Mom played a great role in raising us. As a result of her tremendous effort and hard work, everyone was able to get an education and got good jobs.

CHAPTER 3

Bullies Attempted to Stop Me from Going to School but Failed

I started first grade at Kilimatinde in 1952. At that time, I was seven years old. You may not know this, but during those days in some parts of Africa, to determine if the kid is ready to start first grade, they were asked to extend their hand above the head and touch the bottom of the opposite ear while keeping the head straight. If they could not do that, they were judged as being too young to start first grade. At age seven, I passed that physical test and was allowed to start first grade.

My first and second grade school life was fine. I did well in class and made many friends. But the third year was different. If you think bullying of young kids started recently, you are wrong, my friend. It happened to me in primary school. I did not tell my parents what was happening to me. The funny thing is that what happened then is happening today.

The story is like this. When I was in third grade, a few months after school started, every evening two kids about my age chased me on my way home. The first day when they did that, I thought they just wanted to play with me. But when it started to be confrontational, I realized my life was in danger. Every day when I was in class, I was thinking about the danger I was going to face on my way home. Going to school and learning was not fun anymore. My major problem was that I loved going to school, but how was I going to deal with these two thugs? A solution came unexpectedly.

One day I was going home at the usual time, about three in the afternoon, and I walking along the same route. As I passed the building that was close to the road, the two boys started chasing me. I started running unusually first. They increased their speed in order to catch me. As one of them was about to catch me, I stopped suddenly. Before he knocked me over, I punched him on the side of his face as hard as I could. His friend did not expect I was going to stop, so his head collided with the head of his friend as he was falling after I punched him. This was such a lucky punch. You should have seen me screaming at them at the top of my voice, "Stand up and fight. You think I am scared of you? I am going to teach you a lesson. Come on, fight! They started running while their faces were bleeding. I chased them for a while just to make sure that they realized I was not afraid of them and I was serious about it.

The lesson from what happened to me at third grade is that an individual being bullied will reach a point where he or she can't take it anymore, and a decision has to be made on what to do. In my case, I thought I reached a point where I had to decide to either stop going to school or stop those boys from harassing me. My decision was to continue going to school, and I was lucky to win the fight. But looking back, maybe I should have asked help from my parents or from the class teacher. For all parents, please try to understand your child's behavior. If you note certain acts that make you think he or she might have a character of bullying other kids or being bullied, please provide proper help. Don't wait until it is too late because the price is too high to pay.

Our mother was a strict disciplinarian, focusing on good manners, respecting others, obeying our parents' advice, and working hard at home and at school. The elder brothers and sisters were given the authority to discipline the young ones when they misbehaved or did what they were not supposed to do. The most common punishment was a number of slashes. I know you want to know if I made a mistake or misbehaved and got slashed. Oh yes, a few times. Maintaining a high level of discipline was such a big deal to our parents. They even authorized our neighbors to punish us if we misbehaved in their presence. And then they would report to our parents about what happened for a second punishment.

CHAPTER 4

The Woman Who Wanted to Kill Me

In 1953, Mom and I were on a journey to the district commissioner's office at Manyoni Town. She had four children going to school, and she wanted to ask the district commissioner (a British) to authorize a waiver on school fees for two of them. We got a ride and arrived at Saranda Railway station around 9:30 a.m. where we had to board a train at 12:00 noon to go to Manyoni. The train ride to Manyoni was about one hour. The aim was to be able to talk to the district commissioner before the end of the workday. During colonial era and a few years later, government officers opened at 7:30 a.m. and closed at 2:30 p.m.

At 10:30 a.m., the wife of the railway stationmaster brought cornmeal (in Kiswahili it is called Ugali) with chicken curry and said to my mother, "This food is for your son only, and not for you," and she left. We were both very hungry because we didn't eat breakfast before leaving Kilimatinde. But Mom told me, "We have to throw away this food because I am very suspicious of the lady's intentions. I believe she wants to kill you. Otherwise, there was no reason for asking me not to eat the food. We shall eat in a hotel when we get to

Manyoni." I agreed and Mom put the food under a small rock. About half an hour later, the lady came to us and asked Mom, "How is your son doing? Did he eat that food?" Mom replied, "Oh yah, he was very hungry, but now he feels much better. Thank you very much." She just said, "oh OK" and left. Half an hour before the train arrived, she came and told Mom, "You lied to me. You did not give your child that food." Mom looked at me as if to say, "I told you that food was not safe" and looked at her and said, "I don't know what you are talking about." The lady said "aaah!" and turned around and went back to her home. Mom gave me a big hug and said, "Son, thanks for listening to me and agreeing not to eat that food. There was poison in the food, and her intention was to kill you." Mom thought she was a witch. In any case, Mom saved my life, and for that she is my hero.

In 1954, we moved from Kilimatinde to Kilosa, a small town in Morogoro Region. In Kilosa District, the main tribe is Wakaguru. My parents came from a village called Berega. Therefore, my local tribe is Mkaguru (singular of Wakaguru). In a way, my parents' intention for moving to Kilosa (district capital) was to be closer to home. The weather condition is much better in Morogoro Region compared to Dodoma Region. Our late elder brother, Stanley Chilewa, had a home at Kilosa Town; therefore, he played a big role in helping our parents get established. Within the first year, we had a new home and a farm to grow crops.

I was late to start fourth grade at Kilosa Elementary school; therefore, I was put in the third grade. I registered my name as Dudley Lameck. I used my father's name as my surname. I knew all my siblings use Chilewa as the family name, but I did not see the logic of using Chilewa if my father was Lameck. Chilewa was my father's father, in other words, my grandfather. I thought if I used Lameck, the name identified who my father is. But I accept my identity being Dudley Lameck Chilewa. Few years later, Geoffrey, our last born, changed his last name from Chilewa to Lameck. This was his idea; there was no discussion between me and him. Thirty years later, this was an issue that was discussed in a family meeting.

A repeat of third grade made everything taught in class to be very easy for me. Therefore, I made A's in every subject. The other students thought I was the smartest kid in class. During exams, the teacher had to put my desk at a distance away from other students because whoever was close to me would try to cheat by looking at my answers. During third and fourth grade, I took home all top prices for being the best student in class. My mother was very proud of my educational efforts. Nobody pushed me to work hard in school; I had a natural liking to compete academically with my classmates. I always strived to be number one in class. If a student got a higher grade in a test than me, I would try to find out what he/she did differently in preparing for the test. I would evaluate my learning and studying style and make necessary adjustments. My goal was to get a better grade than the previous test. That technique worked well for me through middle school.

One important part of growing up in our family was helping parents with domestic chores. At the time when I was attending Kilosa Middle school, most of my elder brothers and sisters had moved out and were living independent lives. On top of that, Dad was away on business trips for many months. Therefore, I was the only one around that was old enough to help Mother with whatever assistance she needed. She taught me how to prepare different kinds of dishes, clean the house, wash dishes, clean the laundry, press men's and women's clothes, gardening, and growing different types of crops. I did all types of chores, which, during those days, were done by girls. Mom told me that it was unlikely I would get married as soon as I graduated from college. Therefore, I had be prepared to perform all domestic chores during the first few years of entering the workforce. That would help me to save money instead of going to eat in restaurants every day. Most importantly, when I got married, I would be able to help my wife with domestic chores. She asked me, "Who would cook food for your wife when she is sick?" The other thing she said was "I also think your life would be happier if you helped your wife with domestic chores." But our neighbors complained to Mother for making me perform chores that are normally done by girls. Especially when I carried on my head a bucket full of water. Our house had no plumbing; therefore, we obtained drinking water from an open well. Or sometimes I would go with Mom to the woods and come back carrying a big bundle of firewood on my head. And often they saw me picking fresh vegetables from the family garden. They thought I was being abused. She explained to them that she was preparing me for facing a tough life after I left home. And the fact is, I did not feel I was being abused; actually, I was happy for being able to help Mom deal with everyday chores. Later I will tell you a true story of how I put into practice what Mom taught me.

CHAPTER 5

Other Parents Bought Toy Cars for Their Kids, I Made Toy Cars

Sometimes necessity brings out innovative ideas. When growing up, our parents didn't have extra money to buy toys for us. In developed countries, it is very common for kids to have a variety of toys and a bicycle. I had none of that. But like other kids, I was very energetic and wanted to play. Therefore, following my brother Rhone's footsteps, I made various types of toys, including cars.

I used materials from mature and dry sorghum stalks from the family farm. I selected and used stalks about one and half inches thick, with internodes eight to twelve inches apart. I removed the internodes and the outer cover of the middle part. The inner part was soft and could be made into different shapes using a sharp knife, during the process of building different parts of a car or truck. I made small sharp nails from the outer cover of the stem, which I used for joining pieces of materials to make different parts of the car or truck such as the hood, driver cabin, and the body. I made cars and trucks of different shapes and sizes, depending on the quality of the materials I obtained from the farm. I took discarded old car tire and made small round wheels for my cars and trucks. The size of the wheels I made depended upon the side of the car or truck I was making.

The process of making one car or truck from collecting raw materials to a finished product took about six hours. More time was spent in making the wheels from a piece of a car tire because the rubber material was very hard to cut using a kitchen knife. The next important step was to make the car or truck move by itself on the ground. In order to do that, the car or truck needed some kind of manual power.

I took a piece of rubber band and tied it to the front axle, and the other end I tied to a small stick attached to the outside of the right front wheel. When the small stick was turned clockwise, it tightened the rubber band. Once the car or truck is put on the ground, the rubber band would start to unwind, and that created a force that made the car or truck to move forward. The distance moved would depend on the thickness and the length of the rubber band.

Making moving cars or trucks was a new innovation, which many kids in the neighborhood had never seen before. When they saw the cars and trucks for the first time, they were very impressed. To them it was like a kind of a new invention. I told them, "It is not a big deal. It is just a result of a little imagination."

Our playground became a place for learning to make moving toy cars and trucks. The only bad result was the amount of trash that was being created. When the situation looked like it was getting out of hand, Mother asked me to look for another site for our workshop. The group agreed to move to a new site, and the fun continued.

CHAPTER 6

My Visit to Magubike Village— I Could Not Believe What I Saw

In 1958, when I was in fifth grade, Dad brought his friend's son, Salum Athuman Mwibela (may his soul rest in peace) to live with us. His dad was a local leader at Magubike Village, one of many villages in a big area dominated by Wakaguru tribe. He knew that our family valued discipline, respect, hard work, and most of all, education. Therefore, he thought that if Salum stayed in our family, he would adapt some of the same values, and that would help him get a better life than the one he had at Magubike Village. Our mother accepted Salum to stay with us, but on one condition–he would follow the rules and guidance given to him, like everyone else in the family. When he agreed, he was welcomed as a new member of the Chilewa family. Although Salum and I were the same age, I was a little bigger in size, I guess because of his nutritional deficiencies. He was also two grades behind me. He joined third grade in 1958.

June of 1958, Dad asked Mom if I could go with Salum to Magubike Village to visit his family during school break. There were two reasons Dad had to ask Mom's permission. First, because I did not speak Kikaguru language though I could understand everything said. Second, I had never been in the tribal area before, and in this case, I was going be on my own. Mother was very concerned about my health and what could happen to me. Both Mom and I could remember when some years back a woman at Saranda Railway Station wanted to kill me. At this time, the difference was that there would be no one to protect me. After Dad assured her he would make sure my life would be protected, she allowed me to go. But to say the truth, I was scared too because I did not know what to expect.

Salum's dad sent two strong guys with bicycles to pick us up. The bicycles had seats on the rear wheel with a small pillow. The goal was to make the twelve-hour bicycle ride on a dirt road a little less uncomfortable. We left home at six in the morning and arrived at Magubike Village at six in the evening. My thighs were sore, and I was very tired due to the bumpy ride. I could not imagine going through the same experience when returning home after three weeks. Salum's family was very nice to me, and I had a feeling I would be safe. They had no problem to communicate with me in Kiswahili instead of Kikaguru as they would to my parents or my brothers and sisters.

The following day, Salum asked his dad if he could show me around the neighborhood. His dad agreed but warned us to be very careful. Being in the rural area, the only thing I was worried about was wild animals. On the way to the neighbor's house, Salum assured me that we would be fine. We decided to join a bunch of kids at the cornfield next to the house. I asked Salum, "I see some kids digging something using hand hoes, what is going on?" He looked at me and said, "Does it mean you have never done this before? Oh yah, you grew up in town, I can understand." Up to this point, I had no idea what he was talking about until I saw what they had in the basket. I couldn't believe it was three huge rats. The guys stopped digging as we approached the basket. After greeting them, Salum picked one rat and looked at it and said, "It is dead." I moved backward and screamed, "Don't come close to me, or else you will wish we never met! And I mean it!" When the other guys started laughing, he put the rat back in the basket. I asked him, "What are they going to do with them?" One of the guys in the group proudly said, "We will barbecue them. These are not the same kind as house rats or mouse, they are huge therefore has a lot of meat." I said, "Oh no, where I am coming from, a rat is just a rat, it doesn't matter whether it is tiny or as huge as a goat." I continued, "You guys, have you heard about some kind of birds called chickens? They have more meat and are easy to raise." I went closer to Salum and asked in a very low voice, "You want to tell me when you were staying here you ate this stuff too? I hope you won't tell those guys we will join the barbecue party, whatever you call it. You can go if you want, but not me." He told his friends, "Guys, never mind about him, he is from the town, he is afraid of rats. Keep digging, you might get a few more." He grabbed my left hand and whispered, "Let's go before they get mad, we can't win against a group of seven." We slowly walked away from the cornfield. This was an experience I would never forget.

The next day we joined a group of kids for bicycle riding. It was not the type of bicycles you know, the ones made of metal. In fact that is what I thought too. To my big surprise, they were made out of pieces of timber. They had two wheels about two feet in diameter, connected to a frame shaped like those of metal bicycles and a place to sit. There was a piece of wood attached close to the rear wheel for braking purposes. The only problem was that you could only ride downhill. The rider's weight and the force due to acceleration made it possible to slide down the slope. Of course the riders did not know about physics; for them, what mattered was having fun. Three weeks later, we said good-bye to everyone as we prepared to go back to Kilosa. I told one of the guys, "If you could put a bigger wheel in the front and attach on the sides small pieces of lumber for pedaling, your bicycles can go faster on flat ground." He looked at me and said, "I never thought about that, but it is a great idea worth trying." I said, "Good ideas sometimes can come from someone you just met." He looked at me and smiled.

We left Magubike, going back to Kilosa by bus. I made my mother's day when I told her the story about digging rats for barbecue. She said, "I didn't tell you about that because I never thought they were still doing it. You didn't eat that stuff, did you?" I looked at her and said, "Mom, of course not."

The lesson in the story is that when you are visiting people in an unfamiliar environment, you don't have to take part in everything they do. Especially if you don't like what is going on. Maintain your social values and beliefs without offending the local people. I asked the guys if they heard about chickens. I meant as a joke, but it was a bad joke. I was lucky it didn't result in a fight.

CHAPTER 7

Being a Teenager Is the Beginning of a Journey to Manhood

I mentioned that I grew up in a very poor family of eight siblings. To give you a picture of my childhood life, from first grade to eighth grade, I walked barefoot. My parents did not have extra money to purchase shoes for me. But since all the kids in the neighborhood or my schoolmates were also not wearing shoes, life looked normal. Later, I will tell you when I got my first pair of shoes, but first I want you to learn about Wakaguru tradition and what I went through as a teenager.

During my teenage years, Wakaguru were still practicing circumcision as a passage to manhood. The main purpose is to put teenagers in a camp and teach them about the man's responsibility in the home and in the community. The circumcision was being done to boys between age ten and fifteen years old because at that stage teenagers think they are mature enough to do whatever they would like to do with no consequences. Elders know that when teenagers are in a camp after circumcision, they can't fight. They will respond positively to all commands or do whatever they are asked to do. This does not mean they will be abused because their parents or one of their elder brothers can be among the elders at the camp.

In January of 1961, I was in eighth grade, when one day my dad said, "When you are on vacation in May, you will be circumcised." He continued, "Don't be scared, you will be among a small group of teenagers about your age." I looked at him, thinking, "What do you mean I should not be scared while I have heard terrible stories about what they do to you?" The picture I had in mind is this: somewhere in the bushes, a circle of elders would be singing traditional songs at the top of their voices, and I am at the center screaming as an old man with an ugly face is doing the circumcision using a sharp knife. I asked Dad, "Do I have a choice about this?" He replied, "I am sorry, son, the decision has already been made. I can assure you, everything will be fine." That was the end of the discussion. I will tell you one thing. I wished the month of May would be a hundred years away.

The month of May came, and one evening my dad said, "Tomorrow is the big day. We will go to the hospital early in the morning." In my head I was thinking, "If they won't take me to the bushes, maybe there is no reason to be scared about." That night was the longest night ever. I could not sleep. Throughout the night, I was thinking about what was going to happen to me at the hospital. I wished someone could give me the details of how the circumcision was performed.

My dad woke me up about six in the morning. At six thirty, we were on the way to the hospital in my brother-in-law's car. When we arrived at the hospital, there were four other teenagers with their dads. I was familiar with one of them, though we were not friends. Because I was a year or two older than the other teenagers, I was the first to be sent by my dad into the operation room. Dad asked me to undress my shorts and lie on the operating table and spread my legs. On the side was a small table covered with a clean white cloth, and on top was a container with medical equipment. Two medical assistants stood on either side of the operating table. There was no talking; therefore, I got scared.

A few minutes later a doctor (it was someone I knew) came to the operating table. At that moment, I knew there was nothing I could do except be ready for what was about to happen to my genitals. The doctor saw how scared I was and said, "Relax, you will not feel any pain because I am injecting painkiller medication, but it is better if you don't look at what is going on." At that moment, Dad and one of the medical assistants put a piece of white cloth in front of my face so that I could feel but not see what was going on. In less than ten minutes, it all was over. My dad said, "Good job, son, I am proud of you." Then the doctor told me the dos and don'ts as part of the healing process and promised to visit the group within the next three days and later once a week. They didn't let me put on my shorts; instead, they gave me a piece of cloth to wrap around my west. As I did that, I was thinking, "This is going to be my longest vacation ever."

As we left the hospital, I thought we were going home. Wrong! They took us straight to the camp, which was prepared in advance. Strange enough, I had no idea this camp was about one hundred yards behind our house, close to mango trees. It was made of thick poles and thatched with grass. There were no beds except a small mat on the ground, covered with one piece of cloth and a small pillow. When I saw how the place looked, I thought life for the following four weeks would be completely miserable. At no time in my life I ever thought I would be sleeping on the ground. But there I was, and there was nothing I could do about it. This was our tribal tradition.

As the first order of business, the elder in charge informed us about the kind of life we were going to have for the following four weeks. He also introduced me to the group as their leader and spelled out my responsibilities. One of which was to make sure that the group behaved, practiced high level of discipline, and followed orders. In case they misbehaved, I would be the one that would be punished; then it would be up to me what punishment to give the group. I looked at the group and thought there was nothing they could do that would put me in trouble. A lesson I later learned is, don't prejudge anybody.

There were a variety of topics that were talked about at the camp. From good behavior, man's responsibilities, discipline, respect, working hard, and married life. Nothing was off-limits, including how women act, their feelings, and behavior. One day, as the leader of the elders was emphasizing a point by telling us a story about his friend's

to take us by force from Mom. I thought for a moment and then said, "Mom, you don't have to do this. He won't drag us by force because we will not let him." She looked at me and said, "You know, you just saved your uncle's life. I am very proud of you." I said, "You are our mom, we will do everything to protect you. We don't even know that guy you said was our uncle." "Ha ha ha." She laughed.

CHAPTER 8

Secondary School Education

December 1961, I graduated from Kilosa Middle School. Out of a class of twenty five, I was among five students who passed the national exam and was selected to go to Mzumbe Secondary School in Morogoro. Morogoro Town is the capital city of Morogoro Region. Tanzania got her independence on December 9, 1961. The new government provided free education from first grade to college. Therefore, my parents did not have to pay any tuition for my secondary education or college.

The day I was leaving home to go to boarding school, my dad said, "The good thing about boarding school is that you will get everything you need, a place to sleep and food. I will give you money to buy two stamps. Write to inform us when you arrive at school and to let us know the date you will be coming home for holidays." I was not given pocket money by my dad to spend on stuff I wanted. My dad was a businessman; therefore, he had money, but he just did not want to give me any.

This picture was taken September 1962 during my freshman year. The shoes I was wearing were my first pair ever. Together with everything else, I bought using money I obtained by working part-time at a sisal plantation five miles from Kilosa Town.

If I didn't work at the sisal plantation after graduating from middle school and saved a little bit of money, I wonder what would have happened. Maybe Dad wanted to make sure that I spent the money I had on shoes and uniforms. He knew there was no way I would go to boarding secondary school barefoot and wearing dirty clothes. But this was a big lesson for me, that as far as uniform and pocket money was concerned, I was on my own.

Before the school break in May of 1962, I went to the school library and researched on how to write a job application. I also looked for company addresses, especially those close to home. I thought if I did not work during school break, there was a very high probability I would return to school penniless. I did not want to allow that to happen. I decided to write applications to various companies, asking for a temporary job. All my applications were handwritten because during those years, students or the school didn't have computers. One company responded to my letter and offered me a job. I worked for two months and made some money that enabled me to buy another pair of shoes and a set of uniforms.

For the following three years, I didn't have a relaxing vacation. I had to work in order to get money for buying stuff I needed. Therefore, working during vacations became part of my life. As a result, I valued every penny I made and was able to establish a sense of responsibility and accountability.

At the end of my senior year (November 1965), I did the national exam. During that time, the exam was designed by Cambridge University in Great Britain. Therefore, it was called Cambridge Exam. When results came back from Britain, I got second class. The ranks were as follows first class, second class, third class, and F. Therefore, getting second class was not great, but not bad either.

I applied to attend Morogoro Agricultural College (now Sokoine University of Agriculture). When growing up, I had great interest in farming. I remember one day when I was in fourth grade helping my parents in the vegetable garden, I told them, "I think when I grow up I will be an agricultural officer." At that time, they never took my word seriously. I was very happy when my application was accepted. In January 1966, I joined Morogoro Agriculture College to begin my first year.

CHAPTER 9

Life Was About Making Good Decisions

Life at Morogoro Agricultural College was tough, especially fieldwork. I did not like waking up early in the morning, about 6:00 a.m., to go and work at the dairy farm. Because we were kept so busy with homework, frequent prompt tests, and exams, the first year went so fast.

This picture was taken in July 1966 when I was a freshman at Morogoro Agricultural College. The guy in the center is Aram Mkuchu. We used to sing together in church choir in secondary school. The three of us were from the same tribe, Wakaguru.

In December of 1966, I was among students assigned to go to Iringa Region for agricultural extension practicals. The regional agricultural officer of that region asked the college administration for twenty students to go into villages and measure acreage under pyrethrum crop. Before going to Iringa, I decided to go home to let my parents know where I would be during the month of December and January of 1967. There was a daily train leaving Morogoro at seven thirty in the morning going to Dodoma. Kilosa is on the way to Dodoma, and the train arrived at about eleven in the morning.

Our home was two miles from the railway station. I arrived in about thirty minutes. It was Saturday, so my young brother, my niece, and Mom were both home. Dad was away on a business trip. They were all very surprised and excited to see me because they had no information I was coming home. Mom shouted, "Well, well, this is a nice early Christmas present." To her disappoint, I said, "Sorry, everyone, I won't stay long, I just came to see you before I leave for Iringa Region. Hopefully I will see you again in late January 1967." My young brother, Geoffrey, asked, "With whom are you going to spend Christmas at Iringa that is more important to you than us?" I looked at him, and in a low voice, I said, "It is part of agricultural extension training program. We have to go to farmers' fields and apply what we learn to solve a particular problem." I told Mom we were scheduled to leave by bus from Morogoro the following Friday; therefore, I was going to spend a week with them. She said she had enough time to prepare for me the stuff I would need when I got there.

The day I was leaving, she parked in a medium-sized box the following things: a kerosene cooking stove full of kerosene, a matchbox, five pounds of rice, three pounds of corn flour, a pound of dried vegetables, half a pound of sugar, half a pound of powdered milk, a quarter pound of salt, two cooking pots, three table plates, three soup bowls, three tea cups, a small box of tea packets, two table glasses, a kitchen knife, three pairs of dinnerware. In short, I had everything I needed to cook and serve breakfast or a meal for three people except water. I asked her why she put dinnerware to serve three people. She asked "Son, are you not going to invite friends over during the weekend?" I looked at her and said, "Thanks, Mom, I didn't think about that, you are the best."

The day I left home to go join my college mates at Morogoro Town for a bus trip to Iringa, I had two luggages, a box, and a suitcase. When boarding the bus, one guy, a second-year student and a little muscular than me asked, "Why are you carrying all this stuff? You don't even have a slight idea where they will send you?" I looked at him and replied, "That is exactly the point, I am prepared for wherever they will send me." He didn't ask me more questions; that was the end of the conversation.

When we arrived at Iringa, the regional agricultural development officer gave us the assignment to work in pairs. I was paired with a second-year student whom I never knew before this trip. To make the situation even more interesting, I didn't even know his name, and no introduction was made. Our assignment was to go to Kilolo Village and measure pyrethrum crop acreage. For your information, pyrethrum flowers are crushed and oil is squeezed out. The oil that is produced, which is used as a high-grade botanical insecticide. The crop is produced by small farmers in small plots of about one to two acres. Both of us had never been to Kilolo Village before; therefore, I was prepared for anything we would face.

CHAPTER 10

Life at Kilolo Village

I arrived with my college mate at Kilolo Village on Sunday around 2:30 p.m. We reported to the village chairman. He was at his house, expecting us. As we introduced ourselves to the chairman, I learned for the first time that my partner's name was Isaya. After greetings and a short discussion about the project, he took us to the guesthouse. He showed us around and said, "Welcome to your new home for the next two months. I am at your assistance for anything you might need." We thanked him for the warm hospitality, and then I asked, "Where do we get drinking water, and can we borrow two buckets, please?" He showed us a faucet for obtaining drinking water. It was very close to the guesthouse. The village chairman also said, "In about an hour, my two daughters will bring two buckets of drinking water for you. As he was leaving, Isaya thanked him for the help.

At about five thirty, we saw the village chairman's two beautiful daughters coming to the guesthouse, each carrying a bucket of water. Isaya said, "Oh my, here they come." I looked at him and said, "Don't even think about it, otherwise you will make our life here be miserable." The girls were very shy and polite, a typical behavior of young girls in a small village. After greeting us, they asked where they should put the buckets. I told them to put the buckets in the kitchen, and then I asked, "How much do you charge for each bucket? The older girl said, "There is no charge, you are our guests, and we will try to help you as much as we can." I extended my hand to her and said, "Thank you very much, we appreciate your help." As they turned and started leaving, Isaya said, "Look at that!" I went close to him and whispered to his ear, "You don't get it, do you? If they report to their father what you said, we may be kicked out of the guesthouse. And if you have not noticed, the nearest hotel is twenty miles away, and we have no car. Therefore, if you want to stay in this guesthouse, you better respect our host and his family. I don't think that is too much to ask." Isaya looked at me and said jokingly, "Yes, sir, but may I ask you something? Where are we going to get something to eat?" I said, "Don't you worry, we are fine. Give me one hour, and dinner will be served." I could tell from the look on his face that Isaya had no clue what I was talking about.

After I put the box in the kitchen, I took my suitcase to one of the bedrooms and said, "This is where I will be sleeping for the next two months." I then went back to the kitchen, opened the box, and put the stuff on the kitchen counter. When Isaya saw what was on the kitchen counter, he said, "Damn! Excuse my expression, what I mean is, you are pretty good. How did you come up with such a great idea?" I did not respond to his question. Instead, I asked him, "What do you want for dinner, rice or ugali [fufu]" He looked at me and said, "But I don't know how to cook either dish." I said, "Isaya, did you understand my question? I did not ask you to cook anything. I just wanted to know what you would like to eat for dinner." He thought for a moment and then said, "Dudley, I am not at a restaurant. Decide what you want to prepare, and that will be fine with me." In my mind, I thought, "If I have to cook breakfast, lunch, and dinner every day, this will be the longest two months I ever had." After putting pressure on the kerosene cooking stove, I struck the matchbox to put the fire on. In order to show Isaya that cooking was going to be a collaborative effort, I showed him how to prepare the onions and boil the preserved vegetables. After having done that, he asked, "What else do you want me to do?" I could tell he felt good for helping me prepare dinner. I cooked rice and ugali and let him do the easy things. The next day, we did the same for preparing breakfast and lunch. We also calculated how much each should contribute for buying groceries. Life in the village became a little easier for both of us. You see, the way you plan and execute your first move can have great impact on what you want to achieve. In our case, I was glad meal preparation became a joint effort.

Two weeks later, the village chairman brought another guest to stay at the guesthouse. Since I was coming from a big family, I thought it was not a big deal even though the guy was a little bit older than both of us. He looked like a big brother. The following day, I told Isaya it would be good if we invited the new guy for breakfast, and he agreed. Therefore, we set three cups of tea, toast, and scrambled eggs. The same was for dinner. We set three plates at the table. This went on for three days, and the guy did not show a sign of contributing anything. The fourth day, as were preparing breakfast, I told Isaya, "This has to end. We are students and not a charity organization." Isaya looked at me and asked, "But what are we going to tell him?" I said, "Nothing, but he will get the picture." "I don't understand. What do you mean?" he asked. I replied, "Leave it to me, you will see what I will do. But don't make him think it is a joke. Both of us have to show him we are very serious about what is going on." I told Isaya I was going to set the breakfast table that morning. Instead of setting for three people, I set for only two. There wasn't even a chair for him to sit on. We sat at the table and started eating breakfast. When he came to the dining room and saw what was going on, he turned around and went back to his room. He did not say a word, and neither did we. When we left for work, Isaya asked me, "How the hell did you come up with such a brilliant plan?" I said, "I remember my mom used to say actions speak louder than words. I thought, 'Why not try this trick?' What do you think about the results?" He said, "You know what, he got the message loud and clear, the problem has been solved. He has a choice either to contribute financially or stay away from the dining table." His choice was not to contribute anything and stayed away from the dining table.

Each day after breakfast, we would go to visit villages and measure pyrethrum acreage. At the village, the chairman would introduce us to farmers, and they would show us where their farm begins and ends. Sometimes farmers would prepare lunch for us. Most of them were very friendly. This made our work a whole lot easier. Some of them even prepared local beer for us called ulanzi. It is made by collecting juice from cut suckers of a certain type of bamboo. There was a sad story I would like to tell you about.

One day we visited one farmer for what was now routing for our job. After we measured the acreage of his family farm, he invited us to his home for a drink of ulanzi he had prepared for us. When we got to the house, he asked his wife to serve us with ulanzi. To his great surprise, his wife told him there was no ulanzi to be served. His wife's shameful behavior of hiding a drink he had prepared for his guests made him so angry that his whole body was trembling. He shouted at her, "How dare you hide the drink I prepared for my guests? Shame on you, and I tell you one thing, this is not over and you will pay for it dearly." I told the farmer, "Don't you worry about it, you have a good heart, and what happened is not your fault. We invite you to the guesthouse whenever you have free time." As were going home, we discussed about the incident at the farmer's house. We had an impression that the ulanzi case was not over. And we were right.

The next morning, the farmer came to the guesthouse with his shirt open at the chest and in great pain. We invited him inside and asked what happened to him. He raised his head and pointed to a big burn wound stretching from the neck to his stomach. He said, "My friends, this is what you get when you are married to a crazy woman. As I was sleeping at night, she took a piece of a burning log from the fireplace and stuck it under the bedsheets on my chest to kill me. Can you imagine a person you love and trust doing something like this to you?" I told him we were very sorry for what had happened to him because of our visit to his home. I said, "We invited you yesterday but never thought you would come in this condition." Isaya asked him what he was planning to do after what happened to him. The farmer said he was on the way going to the hospital to be treated and he had decided it was not safe to live with someone who wanted to kill him. The lesson from this incident is that before you are married to someone, do your best to study and understand that person's character, behavior, habit, attitude, and what she/he likes or dislikes. Even after marriage, continue to make great effort to understand your partner because that may help in maintaining a good relationship. The fact is, it is easier to deal with what you know than what you don't know.

We completed our field training at the end of January 1967 after compiling a report on the number of farmers covered at Kilolo Village and the total pyrethrum acreage. This report was sent to the regional agricultural development officer for the Iringa Region. After that, I went back to Morogoro Agricultural College for my second and third year.

CHAPTER II

Partying and Studying Is Sometimes Not a Good Mix

During my third year, my main focus was graduating from college. I spent most of my weekends studying in preparation for the Monday class. One Friday, my roommate asked if I could go with him to visit his friends in town. I agreed as long as we would be back at the campus by 6:30 p.m. in time for dinner in the cafeteria. He assured me that would not be a problem.

Photo: This is me on the right and my roommate,
Douglas Msami, in our dorm room in 1968, our senior year.

We arrived at his friend's home at 3:30 p.m. There were four guys in the living room, drinking beer and listening to loud music. Douglas knew that I didn't drink beer and hated loud music. Therefore, before introducing me to his friends, he asked them to turn the music low. After I was introduced, one of the guys offered me a beer. My roommate came to my rescue by telling them I did not drink beer. The guy responded by saying, "I am sorry, we don't have soft drinks or fruit juice." I said, "It is OK, I am fine." Douglas grabbed a beer from the fridge and started drinking. After two and a half hours, I reminded Douglas that we had to leave in thirty minutes. He looked at his watch and said, "That's OK, at 6:30 p.m. we would be out of here."

To my surprise, at 6:20 p.m., Douglas went to the fridge and grabbed another beer. He did not look at me because he knew I was not happy about it. I did not say a word but made up my mind to leave at 6:30 p.m. as we had planned. At exactly 6:30 p.m., I stood up and said, "Gentlemen, it was nice meeting you, I have to go back to the campus. I will see you next time." Douglas asked me to wait for him to finish drinking his beer, and then we would leave. I told him he could stay there as long as he wanted, but I was leaving. I took a taxi and returned to the campus in time for dinner in the cafeteria.

Another Friday, three months later, he asked me again if I would go with him to visit his friends. I suggested to him we should spend the weekend studying for the Monday class. I said to him, "This is the third week and professor Badii [an Egyptian] has not given a biochemistry test. I think he might give one on Monday. Therefore, we better be prepared for it." He looked at me and asked, "Did he say he was going to give a test on Monday?" I said, "Hey, go and have fun and hope there is no biochemistry test on Monday." He went to visit his friends and came back on Sunday at 9:30 p.m. He was drunk; therefore, he did not study.

Monday morning at 8:00 a.m., professor Badii entered the lecture room with a bundle of papers in his right hand. He said, "Good morning, class" and began handing out the question papers. I looked at Douglas and smiled. In my mind, I knew exactly what he was thinking about. And that is he was going to get an F for this test. In the previous three weeks, we had lectures on amino acid formulas, and that was what the test was about. Some formulas were not easy to remember; you had to memorize. After the test, Douglas came to me and said, "How did you know he was going to give a test today?" I responded, "It was just an easy guess because you know Dr. Badii gives a test after every two weeks. And three weeks passed without a test, therefore, it was time he gave one." The following day, when the results came, I got 92 percent and Douglas got 15 percent out of 100 percent. He said, "I wish I listened to you. If I studied, I would have passed the test." I looked at him and said, "You know, life is about making the right predictions and deciding on your priorities.

After we did a comprehensive exam in November of 1968, we were given forms to complete, indicating our job preferences. My first choice was horticulture and the second choice was agricultural extension education. I graduated and obtained my diploma as an agricultural field officer. During that time, the main employer was the Ministry of Agriculture. When the results of postings came out, I was lucky to get my first choice.

CHAPTER 12

After Graduating from College, the First Six Months

I was twenty-three years old when I graduated from Morogoro Agricultural College. First week of December 1968 when I was on vacation, I received a letter from the principal of the Ministry of Agriculture. There was instruction for me to report immediately for duty at Morogoro Regional Agricultural Office, to be in charge of a national horticultural project. I was so happy and excited to be able to work not very far from home. My parents, especially Mother, was very happy too and wished me the best of luck and success in my new job. For the first time, I was going to be on my own, and I knew from then on whatever decision I would make was going to have an impact on my life. To say the truth, I never expected that right after graduating from college I would be given the responsibility of being in charge of a national horticultural project. I knew this was going to be a great challenge not only on my ability to manage projects, but also on my ability to lead and be successful. I decided that the first thing to do was to obtain as much information as possible about the project and a list of horticultural experts whom I could contact for one-on-one advice.

On Monday of the second week of December 1968, I reported for duty at Morogoro Regional Agricultural Office. After filling the paperwork at the personnel office, I was given the opportunity to see the regional agricultural development officer to discuss about the new national horticultural project. For the first time I learned that the horticultural project was not at the Regional Agricultural Office but was at the Kilombero Agricultural Research Institute (KATRIN) Ifakara District.

I was informed that the Ministry of Agriculture had allocated some funds for a new horticultural project for the purpose of solving nutritional problems due to a lack of adequate vitamins in people's diet. A piece of land next to KATRIN had already been cleared for that purpose. This was a big research center and was being financed by the Tanzania and German government. A new Land Rover and farm equipment had already been sent to the site and three junior staff, two Tanzanians (Peter and Malya), and one Japanese expert (Saito). The emphasis of the discussion was on the fact that I was in charge and responsible for implementing the project goals. The main job of the three junior staff was to assist me to make the project a success. I could hire temporary labor depending on what needs to be done at the farm. At the end of every month, I had to send a report giving details of activities and the progress made. The interesting part was that I was given a typewriter (at that time computers were not very common), an adding machine, printing papers, and payment vouchers, but no secretary or accountant. This meant that I was also responsible for performing office duties. Since I did not know the proper procedure for handling government funds, I decided to ask the chief accountant at the Regional Accounts Office to show me all the things I would be required to do. In life, it is good to know what you don't know and figure out where to go to get help.

The next step was to get good advice on the project from a horticultural expert. Fortunately, at the regional office, there were two horticultural experts, one on growing fruit trees and the other on production of vegetables. Both of them had been at the site; therefore, they were familiar with the land, soil type, and availability of water for irrigation. They also gave me booklets that had very useful information. The other advice they gave me was to go to Ilonga Research Center (Kilosa District in Morogoro Region) and get information from other experts on the best varieties to grow at the site. I thought that was a very good advice because only certain varieties perform well at any given site. I had been to Ilonga Research Center several times years ago; therefore, I knew my way around and who to see to get the information I wanted. It took me two weeks to collect the information I needed for implementing the project and establishing contacts in case I needed help in the future. At this time, I felt I was ready to perform my duties. My mom once told me, "If you present yourself nicely to everyone you come in contact with, there is always a good chance of getting help in case you need it." The following part of my story proved it was a good idea I listened to Mom and followed her advice.

When I arrived at the site, my accommodation was a small round metal house called uniport. It was in January 1969, the weather was so hot during the day, and it was almost impossible to stay inside. Close to the office was a very nice house, but it was already given to Saito. Being the boss and in charge of the project, I could decide either to stay in the same house or ask Saito to vacate. My final decision was that neither was a good idea. I wanted to maintain my dignity as their boss, and I thought being seen by Saito walking around in the house wearing a towel would lower the level of respect. It was a conscious effort from the beginning to establish a high level of conduct because I knew if I didn't, I would not be able to perform my functions as a leader. We were almost the same age, except that I had higher education and more responsibility. There was another thing. Saito, being a Japanese expert, was acting as if he had more authority than me on making certain decisions. I had to do my best not to allow that to happen again. During this time I was single; therefore, I did not care very much the condition of where I slept.

I developed very good working relationship with all my staff and casual workers. Anyone coming to the farm would not know who is the boss unless they asked because I would be working hard and sweating like everybody else. I received a lot of good complements from our causal workers saying that it was the first time they had a boss working hard the way I did. I had three main reasons for working hard: (1) I wanted to be a good example for them, (2) I wanted to motivate them, and (3) I wanted to be able reach the project implementation goals on time.

The first stage of project implantation was going very well. The farm was in three sections: (1) a vegetables section for educating farmers on vegetable production techniques, under the responsibility of Saito, (2) a nursery for citrus seedlings for the farm and some were sold to farmers; Peter was responsible for this section, and (3) an orchard of fruit trees that served as teaching area for farmers under the responsibility of Malya. In April, I was invited by Dr. Hipco, the director of KATRIN Research Center to visit their horticultural section and share some technical advice. I reciprocated the invitation to their horticultural officer. When he came for a visit, he was very impressed with the organization of the farm and the technical aspect of the layout in each section. I did not know that the horticultural officer reported to Dr. Hipco about the stage of implementation of our project until one day when the same officer came to the farm and told me Dr. Hipco wanted to see me as soon as possible. I said, "Fine, tell him I will be at his office tomorrow nine o'clock sharp." As he was leaving the farm, I thought, "What the hell have I done?"

At exactly nine o'clock, I knocked at Dr. Hipco's office door. I heard a deep voice say "Come in." And as I opened the door, I saw this big and muscular middle-aged guy with gray hair and a clean-shaved chin sitting behind a huge and beautiful office table made out of mahogany wood. He said, "Have a seat and make yourself comfortable." While I was sitting down, I was looking around the office and thinking, "I wish one day I had this kind of office, it is very nice." I thought I should make him feel good about his office. So I looked at him and said, "This office looks great." As if he was expecting me to say that, he replied, "Thanks." He immediately asked me, "Did you know why I asked you to come and see me?" I hesitated for a moment and then replied, "No, I have no idea, maybe you can tell me." He said, "We have been watching you and your work since you arrived, and we are very impressed for what you have done so far." I said, "Wow! I had no slightest idea someone was watching what we were doing. But I am glad to hear you like what we have done so far, for us that is very encouraging news." He continued, "We have also noticed that you are staying in a uniport, which is a terrible place for anyone to sleep in. Therefore, we have decided to offer you a house. This house is new, and the furniture is still on the ship coming from Germany. As soon as it arrives, we will set everything and ask you to move in. But I ask you not to inform your government that we offered you a house because if you do, they will deduct rent from you salary. For your information, you will not be charged for water or electricity either. One more thing, your driver will also be given a house where our drivers are staying." I stood up and shook his hand, saying, "Thank you very much for this offer. I appreciate very much your consideration and the decision you made to help me and my driver. This is great news for both of us." He said, "Welcome to KATRIN, and you are invited to community parties that may take place." I responded, "Thanks, and the best of luck in your job." I started leaving, and as I approached the door, I turned and waved to him good-bye.

Many people were surprised to learn that I was offered a house at KATRIN. The reason was that all the twenty-five houses were occupied by research experts from Germany. Although a number of other Tanzanians worked at KATRIN, I was the first and only Tanzanian to be given a house at that research center. Three weeks after my discussion with Dr. Hipco, I passed by the house and saw on the yard the furniture from Germany. The same weekend, I was told I could move in, and I did.

CHAPTER 13

The Fight at the Farm

One day, Saito asked me if the driver of the Land Rover would pick him up from his house every morning to bring him to the office. The distance from his house to the office was less than one hundred yards. I denied his request and told him everybody would use their own means and be at the office on time. There was no exception. He responded by saying a few words in Japanese, and left. Since I did not understand what he said, it didn't matter to me as long as I achieved my goal.

One month later, there was another incident involving Saito, this time with Malya. Saito took, without asking for permission, some of the equipment Malya's group was using. When Malya asked Saito to return the equipment because his group wanted to use them, Saito refused. Malya became so angry that he took a spade and was getting ready to smack Saito with it on the head. I ran to Malya and grabbed his waist to stop him before he was too close to Saito. I told Saito, "You better run because I can't hold him much longer." He took his motorbike and left. Then I said to Malya, "Do you know you were about to create an international incident that would have involved Tanzanian and Japanese governments? It would have been not just about a fight between Malya and Saito, but would have created high-level discussions about the security of Japanese experts in Tanzania. And I don't like to be in the middle of it. In case you have forgotten, I am in charge here. If you have a problem, you have to report to me. Is that understood?" Malya smiled and said, "I am sorry for what happened, but I don't think I can work with that guy." I told him, "Leave that to me. I will talk to Saito about what he did." That evening, I told Saito I wanted to see him at the office. I reminded him about the incident with Malya and said, "I want you to know this. In Tanzania, we don't just grab things if somebody else is using them. We ask for them. Don't ever do that again. If you can't ask your co-workers to lend you one of the equipment they have, let me know I will get it for you."

The following week, there was another incident involving Saito. This time he wrongly calculated the amount of pesticide he applied on the vegetables. As a result, all the vegetables were destroyed. Since the label on the container was in Japanese language, I could not figure out how much he was supposed to apply. I asked him why he did not use pesticides sold in Tanzania or why he didn't ask me for advice on what to buy and where and how much to apply. He didn't answer that question. Because of all those incidents, I thought Saito was becoming a problem and a liability for the success of the project. Therefore, I decided to go to the regional agricultural officer and report what was going on and ask him to either remove him or transfer me to a different place and give me another position. After listening to my story, he decided to remove Saito, which I knew that was what would happen. In May 1969, Saito received a letter asking him to report at the Regional Agricultural Office. Finally, there was peace and tranquility at the farm, and everyone was happy and continued to work hard.

In January of 1970, a team of agricultural officers from the Regional Agricultural Office came to evaluate the implementation of the horticultural project. After three weeks, a report came indicating the project was a success, and I was asked to hand it over to KATRIN Research Center. The letter also directed me to take over the responsibility and the management of extension education programs for Ifakara Subdistrict Agricultural Office. The agricultural officer who was in charge of that office was away for five months, attending national service training. In February 1, 1970, I handed over the horticultural project to KATRIN Research Center and moved from KATRIN to Ifakara Town. I later learned the project farm was named Lameck Shamba. The word "shamba" in English means a farm. Twenty years later, I met a guy from KATRIN, Ifakara. When I told him that I was Lameck, who established Lameck Shamba, he was very surprised. He thought the farm was established by a research officer from Germany.

CHAPTER 14

A Transfer Meant New Assignment and New Responsibilities

In October 1970, the agricultural officer came back from national service; therefore, I was asked to report for a new assignment at the Regional Agricultural Office, Morogoro. My new responsibility was to manage the regional horticultural project. May of 1971, I went to Bunjombora, Arusha, for five months of national service training. I came back in October and reported for duty at the Regional Agricultural Office.

In November of 1971, I was transferred to the Ministry of Agriculture Head Office, Planning Department, Dar es salaam. In October of 1972, I was transferred to Tanga Regional Agricultural Office, where I was given the responsibility of implementing the Tanga Region Horticultural Program. This gave me the opportunity to visit farmers producing fruits and vegetables in all six districts: Tanga, Pangani, Muheza, Korogwe, Handeni, and Lushoto.

While working at the Regional Agricultural Office, I did two things that had never been done before: (1) I developed an empty one-acre plot at an area called Majani Mapana into production of a variety of vegetables: tomatoes, cabbage, eggplant, cauliflower, okra, spinach, and bell peppers. Many people were surprised to see that high-quality vegetables could be produced in an area in the city. I sold the vegetable to government employees at a very reasonable price. (2) In order to leave at the Regional Agricultural Office what I called my signature, I planted in March 1973 a few orange trees on the office yard. My goal was to provide oranges to those working at the office for many years after I was gone. The lesson is this: when you are going away, sometimes it is not very important what you are taking with you, but what you are leaving behind.

The same month, March of 1973, the Regional Agricultural Officer, Mr. Mwaipopo, asked me if I would accept a position of District Agricultural Development Officer for Korogwe District. After briefing me about the problems facing that office, I politely and respectively declined the offer. I told him, "I am sorry about what has happened at Korogwe, but since they created the mess, let them figure out how to clean it." Then, I suggested the names of two Agricultural Field Officers who had worked in Tanga for much longer time than me. He looked at me and said, "I am giving you two weeks to think about it. I really need your help because I think you are the right person to solve the problem." I left his office having made up my mind not to accept the offer.

Two weeks later, he asked me to see him in his office. As I was on the way to see him, I was thinking, "This time there may not be some discussion but an order for me to go to Korogwe." The problem I was facing is this: we knew each other from the time we were both at the Ministry of Agriculture, in Dar es Salaam city. Our offices were next to each other. In many occasions, their telephone calls came to our office, and I was the one going to inform them. Coincidentally, we moved to the Tanga Regional Agricultural Office almost at the same time. Because of the level of respect we had between us, I knew it would be very hard for me to decline his offer for the second time. When I walked into his office he smiled and said "I am sure you know why I asked you to come to my office." I replied, "I think I do." He then told me he made his mind to give me the position, and there was no room for negotiations. He said he was under pressure from the Regional Development Director to send someone to Korogwe as soon as possible. I looked at him for a few seconds and said, "I knew this was coming, so I am not surprised at all." I told him I would go to Korogwe on one condition, that he would commit to give me all the support I was going to need to solve the problems. He smiled and said, "You have my word, and thank you for accepting this position." In February 1974, I moved to Korogwe and took the position of District Agricultural Development Officer.

CHAPTER 15

I Did My Best and Let People Judge Me from the Results

Mr. Mwaipopo, of the Regional Agricultural Development Office, gave me details about the problems facing the District Agricultural Office at Korogwe. Nobody was respecting that office because of the bad behavior of the previous Agricultural Officer. The level of performance of Field Officers and the degree in the implementation of agricultural extension projects was very low. Therefore, I was faced with three major tasks: (1) to restore the integrity of the District Agricultural Office, (2) to improve the degree in the implantation of extension projects, and (3) to establish a good name for myself. I knew this was a great challenge and would not be easy. But I was going to do my very best to solve the problems because for me, failure was always not an option.

The first test came during my first meeting of the District Development Committee. In that meeting, each head of the departments gave quarterly reports on the implementation of development projects. Then, committee members asked questions or clarifications about certain things in the report or just gave comments. After presenting my departmental report, the first question came from one of the ward party leaders. A ward is an area that has five to ten villages, and the leader is called Diwani. He stood up, fumbled through his dirty small notebook, and asked, "Mr. Chairman, I do not agree with the acreage figures presented by the District Agricultural Development Officer. The report I have says there are 3,615 acres of paddy rice, 1150 acres of cotton, and 4,327 acres of maize [corn]. I would like the officer to clarify why there is such a big difference between my report and his." After the chairman gave me the opportunity to respond, I stood up and remained quiet for almost one minute while I looked at every face in the conference room. The room was so quiet you could hear a pin drop. Everyone was waiting anxiously to hear what I was going to say to defend the figures in my report. I heard stories of how they made the previous Agricultural Officer very uncomfortable during such meetings. In my mind, I thought, "Oh hell, they are barking at the wrong tree." I decided this was the time to introduce myself, and after the meeting, everyone would know there is a new sheriff in town.

I looked at the Diwani, who was waiting for my answer, and asked him, "In order to make sure we are speaking on the same terms, is your report in acres or hectares? And do you know the difference between an acre and a hectare?" I was hoping he would say he didn't know the difference because that would really make my day. And just as I thought, his reply was "No, I don't know, is there a difference?" When I heard that answer, I felt my blood pressure going up due to the building up of my emotion. I looked at the chairman and then looked at the members in the hall, and then said, "You see, Mr. Chairman, the problem is not that the figures in my report are wrong, the real problem is we are talking about the same thing in different terms, and this member does not understand that." My report was in hectares, and his was in acres, these were two types of units that were not the same. His question should have been, "What do you mean by the term hectare?" I continued by saying, "For some time now, Tanzania has been using a metric system. And for the benefit of all committee members, 2.5 acres makes one hectare. Therefore, if he wants to convert his acres into hectares all he has to do is divide his figures by 2.5."

I made up my mind to take this opportunity to address the long-term problem. In order for everyone to pay attention, I raised my voice and started to speak with authority. I began by saying "Everyone in this room is a leader and is accountable to the people who pay their salaries. They did not send us in here to spend time challenging each other on things that has no basis. They trust that when you are advising them you know what you are talking about. And if you don't, you would take the proper approach to ask someone who is an expert in that field. The point is, we are supposed to work together in solving problems, and that is what the people in the villages expect us to do. The leaders at all levels must function as one team in the implementation of rural development projects. For our team to succeed, every member has to play their role effectively. I hope everyone will leave this hall with a new sense of collaboration and not confrontation. Because that is what is expected we would do. Our people want to see positive results as far as improving rural life is concerned. And we have an obligation to do our level best to deliver that by working together. We meet in this hall to share ideas and provide good suggestions on how we can achieve our goals." I paused for a few seconds and asked, "Mr. Chairman, is there anybody else with a question?" The chairman said, "Eh, he! This is the best speech I have ever heard during this type of meetings. I hope everyone has understood what has been said. Is there anybody with a question?" When nobody raised a hand to ask a question, he said, "I thought so." Then he announced the meeting was adjourned until next time.

As I was sitting down, the District Land Development Officer who sat next to me whispered to me, "That was a great speech, I am glad you spoke on behalf of all heads of departments. These meetings sometimes turn ugly. I hope from now on committee members will refrain from confrontation, and there will be good collaboration in the implementation of rural development projects." I said, "I hope so."

My speech came as a surprise to everyone and especially the committee members who were much older than me. Many of the Diwani leaders were the same age as my father. They could not believe I had the courage to talk to them in a voice that commanded some authority, and no one challenged me. When the hall was dead silent, that made me believe everyone was paying attention. That was the reason I kept talking. I thought they understood and supported the points I was making. At the time when committee members were getting out of the hall, I found the Diwani who asked the question waiting for me at the entrance door. He extended his hand to me and said, "I like what you said about working as a team and to increase our collaboration in implementing rural development projects." He then asked, "When are you coming to my area to check on the irrigation projects?" When I heard him say that, I realized the speech was worth every minute of it, but I never thought I would see the results so soon. I shook his hand and smiled and then said, "You have got a deal, my friend, what about this coming Monday? After all, today is Friday. I will be at the village office at ten in the morning." He replied, "You know what, I already like you. I will tell you why. It is because you tell people what you think is the right approach to work together. I will see you on Monday, have a nice weekend." The point I would like my readers to take from this part of my story is that don't let anyone intimidate you in performing your duties as long as you know you are doing the right thing. And you have to find ways to get the collaboration of others so that the outcome becomes the result of a team effort. Your main goal should be to get the job or project completed on time and at a high level of satisfaction.

CHAPTER 16

A Visit to the Diwani's Village

After the meeting, I asked the District Land Development Officer if he could accompany me to pay a visit to Diwani's village to evaluate the progress made on the implementation of three irrigation projects. I told him jokingly, "You know, after the way I responded to his question, I feel like I needed a bodyguard during my visit to his village." He looked at me and asked, "What do you think he might do to you?" He shook his head and said in a low voice, "He is not that stupid to do anything that would kill you because he knows the police will figure out who killed you. And people at his age are usually afraid to go to jail. But if you insist, I will go with you. After all, it is almost a month since I went to that village." The main reason for asking this officer to go with me was not only to show the Diwani we were working as a team, but also to avoid any surprises.

We arrived at the village on time, and in the office were three members of the village council and the Diwani. After a long discussion about the implementation of three irrigation projects, we went to the irrigation sites. The paddy rice in the irrigated fields looked splendid. There were few areas of the irrigation channels that needed some repairs. At the site, we also discussed about the next crop to be planted after harvesting paddy rice and came to the conclusion that farmers should be advised to plant field beans and vegetables. As we were leaving the irrigation site at about 1:30 p.m. going back to the village office, the Diwani said, "I would like to invite you to my house, and maybe we can have something for lunch." At this moment, I recalled in my mind the Friday's conversation I had with District Land Development Officer and my looks toward him indicated I needed his approval. When he nodded his head, I replied to the Diwani, "Thanks, that is very kind of you." We went to his house and found he prepared a very nice lunch for us, the kind of lunch made for special guests. In the village, such a lunch consists of steamed and spiced rice mixed with goat or cow meat. It is called pilau, served with African salad called kachumbali. The Diwani asked if he could serve us beer. I told him, "No thanks, you know we are not allowed to drink beer while we are still on duty. But if you are done for today go ahead have some beer." After having lunch, I thanked our host, the Diwani, and then we went to the village office to sign the visitor's book and write our comments about the irrigation projects. As we were on our way back to Korogwe, the District Land Development Officer looked at me and said, "How come I have never been invited by Diwani to his house, have a special dinner, and get an offer for a beer? Maybe we should plan to start going together on our field trips." I smiled, and after a small pause, I said, "You know what, I really don't mind doing that." The lesson here is that whatever your position is, always do your best in performing your duties. Someone will notice your work ethics, and good things may start happening to you.

The speech at the meeting had a positive effect in changing people's perception of the District Agricultural Office. There was a general improvement in the collaboration among leaders in the implementation of rural development projects. Let me lay out to you how agricultural production was in Korogwe District when I took over the position of district agricultural development officer.

Korogwe District is on a major highway going to Moshi and Arusha. There is a stretch of about fifty miles where travelers see farmers' fields on both sides of the road. During the rainy season, between March and May, fields would have corn or cotton. Travelers have firsthand opportunity to see the type of agricultural practices farmers used. I moved to Korogwe at the end of March 1974, which was the beginning of the planting season. Along the highway, I noticed that maize and cotton crops were not planted in proper spacing. After visiting a number of villages, I also found out that very few farmers used hybrid seeds and fertilizers on their farms. I then decided that my first priority would be advising farmers to grow crops using proper spacing and applying fertilizers. I knew if farmers planted crops using proper spacing and controlled weeds in time, and if rainfall was adequate, this would double their yields. I spent a lot of time during the first year training my field staff on educating farmers to grow their crops using proper spacing and the application of fertilizers. In March of 1975, at the beginning of planting season, my field staff held demonstrations in many villages, showing farmers proper spacing and the use of fertilizers on cotton, paddy rice, and maize crops. I emphasized to them to make sure that all farms along the highway were planted using proper spacing. The site of these farms gave travelers the good impression of the type of practices farmers in Korogwe District used for crop production. The season started with good rain, and many farmers planted their crops according to the instructions they were given by field staff. The appearance of crops in every farm was terrific. The change in crop production techniques was a great a success. By March 1975, Korogwe District had eleven irrigation projects. There was also an increase in the production of maize, cotton, and paddy rice. Around May of 1975, a terrible incident happened involving one of my field agricultural assistants. The story is in the following chapter.

CHAPTER 17

Some Problems Are Just Unpredictable

One Monday morning in May 1975, Mr. Nicolas Kihiyo, Assistant Field Officer for Mombo Division, came to my office with some bad news. He told me one of his support staff who lived at Mombo Village had died. He said, "Sir, the worst part is that he has already been buried, and I did not have any information that he was sick." I asked Nicolas, "What are you talking about, and who was the sick guy you didn't know about? Nicolas replied, "Sir, it was Mohamed." I asked for a full story as to what happened to Mohamed and why he didn't know he was sick and why I was also not informed. The bigger question was whether his family knew he was sick and if they were involved in burying his body. The answer was no, they didn't have any information about Mohamed. This was the situation I was in: one of my staff got sick, he was buried, and his family had no information. The question I had was "Where was I going to start?" The problem I had was the cultural and traditional difference between my tribe and that of Mohamed. I was from Kilosa District, Morogoro Region, and my tribe was Mkaguru. Mohamed was from Handeni District, Tanga Region, and his tribe was Mzigua. I had no idea about Wazigua cultures and traditions concerning handling of a sick relative and burial matters. To complicate matters more, I did not know whether Mohamed was married or in which part of Handeni his family was. I had no choice but to depend on Nicolas to help me solve Mohamed's case. Therefore, I told Nicolas we were going to start our investigation about Mohamed from where he lived. And we would follow all stages of his treatment and find out what killed him and why he was buried without informing his family or our office.

Nicolas told me he knew for a long time that Mohamed was not living with his family, but had a girlfriend. His family was in a village in Handeni District, some ninety miles from Korogwe. Now the situation was becoming very interesting but at the same time scary. It meant that there was a very high probability his family did not know that he became sick, died, and was already buried. I was thinking, "How are we going to tell his family that Mohamed is dead but we don't have the body because he has already been buried." I told Nicolas that we were going to solve the case, but we had to get all the facts in detail because his family would like to know what happened to Mohamed and what actions we took.

I came to find out that Mohamed's girlfriend's job was making and selling local beer. Obviously, Mohamed was not only her boyfriend but was also her customer who got free beer. One Friday, Mohamed got sick from stomach diarrhea. His girlfriend took him to Mombo dispensary for treatment. We went to talk to the doctor at the dispensary. He showed us the report and the date Mohamed was admitted for treatment of acute diarrhea. He said he was so sick, and since could not offer the required treatment, he transferred him to the district hospital at Korogwe Town. We went to see Dr. Elexander, the district medical officer. I knew Dr. Alexander because we both attend district committee development meetings. After he invited us into his office, I asked him if he was aware of a seek person that was transferred from Mombo dispensary to his hospital. He said, "Oh yah, he was suffering from acute diarrhea." I pretended as if we had no information that he was dead. I asked him, "Please, would you mind to take us to see him?"

Dr. Alexander said, "He is dead, actually he died four days ago." I looked at him as if I was surprised to hear that. I asked, "You mean to tell us his body has already been taken by his family?" He said at a very low voice, "I am very sorry to say that nobody turned up to claim the body. Because our mortuary is not refrigerated, our policy is if that happens, after three days we bury the body at the common burial ground." I stood up and said, "No! are you sure you are talking about Mohamed? I think you buried a different person, not him. Check your records." He showed me the hospital record that indicated that Mohamed died of acute diarrhea at 1:00 p.m. on Sunday and was buried Thursday morning at 10:00 a.m. I asked Dr. Alexander, "What am I supposed to tell his wife and kids? You want me to tell his parents, brothers, sister, uncles, and in-laws that Mohamed had just disappeared?" I continued, "By the way, do you know which grave he was buried into in case they may want to get the body?" Dr. Elexander replied, "No I don't, and I would not recommend to you to get the body, it will be in a very bad shape." I asked the doctor to provide us with a death certificate so that we could send it to Mohamed's family. After handing over the certificate to me, he jokingly said, "Good luck." I looked at him and replied, "Thanks, I am sure I would need a lot of that."

As we were leaving the hospital, I asked Nicolas, "Suppose we tell Mohamed's family that he is dead and has already been buried, they don't believe us. And then they ask to have proof of a body, are we going to dig up the body from the grave? The fact is, the hospital doesn't bury bodies in a coffin. I could not imagine the scene of digging out the body buried for more than a week." Nicolas said, "There is a very good possibility that would not be necessary if they are told the whole story about what happened to Mohamed." I asked him, "Do you think you can do that?" He said, "Oh yah, I am ready to deliver the bad news to his family." I gave Nicolas the departmental Land Rover and two junior staff to accompany him to take Mohamed's stuff and deliver the bad news to his family. I told them that they should not go directly to Mohamed's family. Instead they should follow traditional ways of handling such sensitive matters. We agreed that once they got to the village, they would brief the information to one elder who knew the family well. They would then go the family and the elder would deliver the bad news. One thing that made the handling of this case a little easy was that Mohamed was not very close to his family. In fact, before his death, he had not seen his wife and children for many years. Therefore, his passing away did not make his family feel a big loss of someone they loved or depended on for financial support.

The lesson from this story is that what you learn in college does not prepare you on how to handle every situation you would encounter in life. But college education prepares you in how to think positively, how to collect proper information, and how to analyze it to solve the problem at hand. The following story is about another incident that happened while I was the district agricultural development officer of Korogwe District. Because of one person's lie, a number of people almost lost their lives.

CHAPTER 18

I Took All Necessary Precautions to Save Lives

Early March of 1976, my office bought several bags of maize hybrid seed as part of implementing rural development project. This seed had already been mixed with a pesticide called Fernasan-D, for preservation. The goal was to distribute the seed to selected villages in the project area, in preparation for the planting season. For precautionary purposes, I also prepared and distributed to the villages warning information written (in Kiswahili) in red ink about the danger of eating the seed. When translated in English, the information said, **"WARNING: the seed is strictly for planting. It is mixed with a pesticide called Fernasan-D which is very poisonous. Therefore the seed should not be eaten by humans or fed to livestock."**

I delivered twenty bags of maize seeds, each weighing ninety pounds at Magamba Kwalukonge Village, with the warning notice. This village is a few miles from Mombo Town. I also discussed with the village leader about making sure that the warning information reached everybody in the village. I said to him, "You and everyone else should take this information very seriously. Anybody who will eat the maize from these bags will get sick and may die. I am not going to be responsible if someone ignores the warning and gets sick after eating the maize meant for planting only." The village chairman assured me he would inform everybody about the warning. After writing my comments in the visitor's book, I signed and left.

A few days later, I received a call from Nicolas, the field agricultural officer stationed at Mombo. He said, "Sir, you better come right away because I have just received information from the ward secretary that a number of people are getting sick at Mzinga and other villages. It appears the sickness is due to something they ate, and I have no idea what it might be. But the ward secretary is giving them milk and take them in a truck to Mombo dispensary for treatment of vomiting and diarrhea." When he told me what was going on, I immediately knew the people who were getting sick must have eaten the seed treated with pesticide. But the question was, who gave them the maize seeds? Why didn't he follow the warning information, and what was going to be the consequences?

As I was preparing to leave my office to go to Mombo, I received a call from the District Development Director, asking me to go to his office immediately. I knew he must have received the news about people getting sick. As I approached his office, I saw him standing at the door. He said, "We need to go to the District Commissioner's office, he is waiting to have a meeting with us." I knew then that we were facing a crisis because it was very unusual to have an impromptu meeting with the District Commissioner. After the security guard let us in, the District Commissioner asked me, "Have you heard the news about people getting sick in the Mombo area?" I replied, "Yes, sir, I was about to go there when the District Development Director asked me to go to his office. But I don't have the details yet." He said, "The reason I called both of you is that the information I got says someone went to Magamba Kwalukonge Village and bought a few bags of maize pretending to go and sell as seed. But instead, he put the maize through his maize mill to make maize flour and sold it to people in three villages. After eating the food made from the maize flour, they all started vomiting and having diarrhea. The quick reaction by the ward secretary of giving them milk and taking them to Mombo dispensary saved many lives. I want both of us to go there and find out what exactly happened and who is responsible."

When I saw the District Development Director looking at me, I knew he wanted me to say something. I began by saying, "A few days ago, I sent twenty bags of maize seeds to Magamba Kwalukonge. I gave the village leadership the warning instructions indicating that the maize is treated with a pesticide called Fernasan-D and should not be eaten by humans or fed to livestock. I discussed the warning information with them and said they should make sure everybody in the village got the information. They assured me they were going to do that. I think what happened was that a businessman might have lied to the village chairman, pretending to buy the maize seed to sell to farmers in other villages. But his goal was to sell maize flour because he would make more money. We will get all the information when we visit Magamba Kwalukonge." The district commissioner looked at both of us and said, "OK, let's go."

We passed by Mombo Town to pick the divisional secretary responsible for Magamba Kwalukonge and other villages. On the way to the village, the District Commissioner asked the divisional secretary to tell us what he knew so far about the incident. He told us the same story we already knew. But he could not answer a key question of who authorized the sell of the maize seeds to the businessman. And was he warned that the maize was for seed only, and if consumed by humans or animals they would get sick or even die? He didn't have an answer to that question. Getting these answers was key to the investigation. Therefore, we continued our journey to Magamba Kwalukonge Village.

When we arrived at the village, the chairman and the secretary were in the office. After we were invited in, the District Commissioner started inquiring about the report of people getting sick. He especially wanted to know if Magamba Kwalukonge Village was involved in selling maize seeds to people from other villages and if there were any specific instructions given to whoever bought the maize seeds. The village secretary pulled a folder from the table drawer, and as he handed it over to the District Commissioner, he said, "This is the information we got from the District Agricultural Officer when he brought the maize seed. It was a warning about not to eat the seeds or feed to livestock. This information was given to everyone, including the merchant who came to buy maize seeds on behalf of the people in his village. But we later found out that he lied to us. He sent the maize seed to his maize mill and made maize flour, which he sold to people in a number of villages. Therefore, sir, that merchant is the one that caused the problem, and he should be prosecuted for selling poisonous food material to people. The Agricultural Officer did everything right, just the way it was supposed to be. We appreciate very much his effort."

The District Commissioner looked at me and said, "I know he is doing a good job, but we need to get this merchant and bring him to justice for what he has done to so many innocent people. But I will now hand over the task of finding and prosecuting the merchant to law enforcement officers." At that point, our investigation was done, and we went back to Korogwe. The police was informed about the incident and was able to bring the merchant to justice. The main point in this story is that you should always do your part of the job right in case somewhere along the line someone else screws-up. Your role in doing that job is protected.

CHAPTER 19

The Trip I Almost Never Made

One day in May 1975, I received a telephone call from Mwaipopo, the Regional Agricultural Officer in Tanga, to see him at his office the following day. He told me there was an important issue he wanted to discuss with me, and he did not want to do it on the phone. I agreed to go to see him, but that night I could not sleep well because I was not sure what the issue was.

I knocked at his office door at 8:00 a.m. As I was approaching the visitors' chair, he said, "I am glad you came. Sit down, there is something very important I want to tell you about. By the way, how are things going in Korogwe?" I said everything was going on well and asked, "What is it that you want us to discuss?" He said, "There is a letter from the Ministry of Agriculture for a study tour to Cimmyt Research Center in Mexico. That center is famous for doing research on improved varieties of maize and wheat. The letter specifies that we need to send a Field Agricultural Officer [FAO], but the personnel officer wants to send an Assistant Agricultural Officer [AFO], simply because they are from the same tribe. I am not going to allow that to happen. I want to make sure we are sending a qualified person as specified in the letter. That is why I called you because you have far more than the desired qualification."

I asked him if the other guy (the person I knew) had already been notified about the study tour. He looked at me and said, "I don't think so, but I don't care because I have the responsibility of making the final decision. This is not supposed to be a shopping trip. I am sending someone I know will bring knowledge that would benefit the people of this region. And that is going to be you." I said, "Well, send me an official letter and the details, and I will be on my way to Mexico." He wanted to know who will be in charge of my office when I was gone. I told him Mr. Kaaya, my assistant, was competent to do the job. He said, "Expect to get an official letter within the next two weeks, but meanwhile, don't tell anyone about our discussion." I assured him what was discussed in the office remained between us. I asked him if there was anything else he wanted to tell me. He said that was it. I stood up, extended my right hand, and said, "Thank you very much for making the right decision. I will keep you posted about the study tour." As I approached the office door, I turned and waved good-bye.

During the second week of May 1976, I received the official letter with details for the study tour to Mexico. I had one week and a half to prepare for the trip. Knowing the type of bureaucracy I had to go through, that was very little time to be able to process everything. First I had to get a letter from the Ministry of Agriculture giving me permission to go. After getting clearance from the Income Tax Department, I needed another letter from the Ministry of Labor and Personnel to send to the Ministry of Treasury to request for foreign funds for pocket money. The last two stages were equally very important. First I had to get a passport and then the Mexican visa. I also had to do all the needed inoculation at the Health Department before the trip date. Having worked at the Ministry of Agriculture before was a big help because I knew a number of officers who could help me. And I lived in Dar es Salaam for two years before I was transferred to Tanga Region; therefore, I was familiar with the location of most departments. One day before the trip, I met the other three guys at the Ministry of Agriculture. We had all accomplished all the preparations and were ready to travel.

CHAPTER 20

My First Trip Overseas Was Quite an Adventure

We left early July 1976 on Sunday by British Airways jumbo jet at 10:45 p.m. This was my first time to travel by plane, and as you can imagine, I was afraid about flying. I could not sleep throughout the flight. We arrived at London Heathrow Airport early Monday morning. Our connecting flight was about an hour later. One airport worker helped us go through the customs section and walk on the moving plastic belt and took us to the other British Airways counter for checking in. Without his help, we would have missed our flight to John F. Kennedy Airport, New York City, USA. By 9:00 a.m., we were on the way to New York.

We arrived at John F. Kennedy International Airport in New York at about two in the afternoon. Our tickets showed our next flight would be Mexican Airways at 6:00 p.m. We decided to spend three hours visiting department stores in New City. Therefore we took a taxi and asked the driver to take us to the nearest department stores. After he took us to the city, before he left, I asked for his business card. I told him we would call him after three hours to take us back to the airport.

We went into the closest department store. The place was full of customers. We noticed some were getting into a sliding staircase going to the second floor. This was the first time we saw a moving staircase; therefore, we had to watch other customers in order to learn how to use it. After a few minutes, I moved closer, and as the next stair was above the floor, I stepped on it while I grabbed the top of the side short wall. As I was moving up, I looked back at the other guys and made a hand signal telling them to follow my lead. When we were both on the second floor, I said, "This is New York, my friends, we are in the United States." We went from one store to the next but didn't buy anything. We had very little money, and we were not sure when we were going to get our next allowance checks. And even worse, we didn't know how much the amount was going to be. At 4:00 p.m., I called the taxi to take us to the airport. Our flight to Mexico City left on time.

We arrived at Mexico City airport before midnight. There was nobody from Cimmyt Research Center at the airport to welcome us. We realized that very few airport workers spoke English, and none among us spoke Spanish. After about an hour, and after talking to more than ten people, one worker said something, and we heard the word "informacion" as he was pointing to an office. I said to the other guys, "I think he was showing us the information office. Let us go we may get help there." The person at the information office spoke good English and was very helpful.

He gave us the name of a hotel where we had to spend the rest of the night. Close to that hotel, we would catch a bus going to Cimmyt Research Center next morning at 7:00 a.m. But he emphasized to be at the bus stop not later than 7:00 a.m. because he was not sure there would be another bus after that time. I looked at him and said, "Sir, thanks for that information, but we don't know where that hotel is and how to get there. Would you please call the safest taxi in the city to take us to that hotel? It would be nice if he can speak some English. We wouldn't want to end up in a dark alley of Mexico surrounded by a bunch of who knows what." He laughed and said, "Don't worry, you will be safe. I know you would do the same if I visited Tanzania." I responded, "Oh sure, we will give you all the assistance you might need to make your stay comfortable and enjoyable." The taxi driver was a very nice guy. And as a result, we gave him a very good tip.

At Cimmyt, we were organized into two groups. One group was for those who spoke English, and the other group for Spanish speakers, but we shared the lecture hall. During every lecture, there was another researcher as an interpreter. During trips to field sites, we travelled in two separate buses. Once every two weeks, we went to Poza Rica in Santa Cruz, at the eastern coast of Mexico, for field training. This involved big plots in farmers' maize fields.

Photo: August 1976. A plot of maize in the local farmer's Field in Poza Rica, Santa Cruz, Mexico.

The reason for having maize plots in Poza Rica was mainly due to warm climatic condition, similar to the countries where trainees came from. Small local farmers were involved in the study to show that if they could adopt improved practices, that meant small farmers in other developing countries in the tropics could do the same.

The discussion at this maize field was on how to control the damage on maize caused by rodents and underground insects. In the picture, the guy on the left side was from Guatemala, the guy in the center wearing a cap was from Haiti, and the guy close to me was from Costa Rica.

One Saturday two months later, we decided to go shopping in Mexico City. By this time we could speak a few Spanish words we learned from a pocket-size English-Spanish phrase dictionary, enough to be able to give or respond to a greeting, bargain for a cheaper price, or order the right type of meal in a restaurant. We thought we acquired enough Spanish to be able to get around in the city. By the way, what would we tell people back home about Mexico if we never went to the city center?

We took a bus ride to the city center. In 1976, the population in Mexico was about nine million people. Compared to Dar es Salaam, then the capital city of Tanzania, we thought Mexico City was very crowded and had too much traffic. One time we had to ask the traffic police to blow his whistle to stop the traffic so that we could cross a busy street. He looked at us, smiled, and then blew his whistle, extending his right hand to stop the traffic while giving us a signal with his left hand to cross the street. I thought that was pretty cool.

As we stood at the end of a street near a big building, one Mexican guy came to us and asked in English, "Guys, do you want to buy stuff real cheap? Follow me, I will show you." We stood there in complete silence for few minutes, trying to think how we were going to respond. First, we didn't know what kind of stuff he was talking about. Second, we were afraid he might take us to a drug dealer. Or was it a trick to get us robbed by a gang? When he saw that we were not following him, he said, "Guys, trust me, it is OK. I just want to show you the open marketplace. But make sure you don't stay too long." We looked at each other, and I said to the guys, "Well, you wanted to see Mexico City, then what are you waiting for?" We followed the Mexican guy, but at a distance.

The open marketplace was full of people selling all kinds of merchandise at very good prices. We all bought a few items, and then we heard someone shouting, "Police, police." People started to run in all different directions. As we started to run, I said, "We better stay together. If anything happens, we would be stronger as a team to deal with it." After two blocks, we decided it would be safe to take a taxi and go to the bus stop for a ride back to Cimmyt. That was the end of the Mexico City adventure.

Our study tour was completed at the end of October 1976. We boarded a Mexican Airways flight to John F. Kennedy, New York, USA. Our connecting flight was again British Airways via London, Heathrow Airport, where we boarded another connecting flight to Dar es Salaam, Tanzania. I arrived at Korogwe Town on Saturday evening, ready to resume working on Monday.

CHAPTER 21

What a Great Surprise, My Assistant Was Gone

When I went to the office on Monday morning, I was told by the office accountant that Mr. Kaaya, who was my assistant, was no longer with us. I asked him, "What do you mean? Did he quit the job or was he fired?" He asked in a very low voice, "Didn't you get the bad news? He died two months ago." I screamed, "What! No! It can't be! He was very healthy and quite strong when I left. What happened to him?" He answered, "He died from stomach ulcers. He was first admitted to the district hospital. After three days, he was sent to the regional hospital in Tanga where, two days later, he died." I said, "This is a great surprise to me because I didn't know anything about him being sick. It seemed as if people didn't want me know until I was back. I don't like this." When I asked the accountant who was in charge of office activities after Kayaa died, he said, "The guy who was head of the mechanization program took over the office responsibilities." I immediately told him, "I can sense things are in a mess. The reason I didn't give him the position of assisting me is because I didn't trust him." I told the accountant to give me all the information on funds spent, stuff bought and delivered to villages, including amount of diesel for the mechanization project.

I came to find out that sixty bags of high-quality paddy rice seed under a rural development project were bought but were not delivered to the village. Nobody could give me information on what happened to the sixty bags of paddy seed. My assumption was that someone sold the sixty bags and put the money in his pocket.

The same thing happened for the mechanization project. When I visited all the villages listed under the mechanization project, the village leaders assured me that the project tractor was not sent to their village. This meant that thousands of liters of diesel were purchased by local purchase order (LPO) but disappeared. I went to get more information from the gas station where we purchased diesel by LPO. I asked the owner to tell me the truth; otherwise, he would also be in big trouble because I had all the information I needed to open a fraudulent case. He said the guy in charge of the mechanization project sent an LPO to purchase diesel, but instead, he asked to get cash. Then I asked him, "How much did he give you for each purchase?" He said, "Twenty percent." I asked for all copies of the LPOs, made copies, and sent them to the police station for legal action.

At the time, when I was carrying out the investigation, the guy in charge of the mechanization project disappeared. For months, nobody seemed to know where he went. One morning, I received a call from the District Development Director, saying that he saw the guy we were looking for in Dar es Salaam City. I asked him, "Did you report him to the police?" He said, "No, I didn't." I asked him, "Why not? You knew we were looking for him because he had a case." To my surprise, he said, "I was afraid if they put him in jail his friends would come after me." In my mind, I was thinking, "There is a high probability this guy knew what was going on, and now he does not want to be involved. Maybe because he is afraid he might be called as a witness." To make the story short, that was the end of the case on mismanagement of public funds.

CHAPTER 22

Doing My Very Best Helped in Protecting My Job

One Monday morning, the phone rang as soon as I entered my office at about 7:30 a.m. When I answered the call, the voice on the other side asked, "When was the last time you visited Magamba Kwalukonge Village?" I recognized the voice. It was that of the District Development Director. I responded by saying, "Is that your greeting to someone? Would it have made a big difference if you first said good morning? Frankly, I don't think so." He said, "You may not know this, but the president, Julius Kambarage Nyerere [the first President for Tanzania], is coming to Tanga Region, and he is scheduled to visit Korogwe District." I replied, "How would I have known that if I was not invited to the meeting?" He continued, "One of the villages he is going to visit is Magamba Kwalukonge." I asked, "So what is the problem with that?"

Of course I was aware that the village farm was in a mess, and I knew who caused the problem, but he didn't. My response made him mad. "This is very serious stuff. You think it is a joke?" I said, "You are the one who make it sound like a joke. How could you plan for the president to visit a village which you don't have current information about? Why didn't you discuss with me about possible villages for the president visit before you went to the meeting?" He responded by saying "There is no point of discussing about that now." I asked him, "Do we have to show the president only the good stuff? Why don't we show him also areas where he can help in motivating the people in the villages?" He quickly responded by asking "You want me to get fired? You will be the first to go before I do." I said, "Is that a threat to my job? If I were you, I wouldn't even try to mess with someone I know very little about. If you don't believe me, be my guest and try, you will see the results." He said, "We shall see. But for now get ready to go to Magamba Kwalukonge Village. I want to get to the bottom of this." I told him, "I will be waiting for you outside my office." Five minutes later, we were on the way to Mombo Town to pick the divisional secretary and then proceeded to Magamba Kwalukonge Village.

The problem at Magamba Kwa Lukonge was caused by the divisional secretary. He made a decision without consulting with me, which resulted in a big mess. In January of 1977, I had discussions with village leaders of Magamba Kwalukonge about planting composite variety of maize and applying NPK type of fertilizer. The plan was that I would send a tractor, a planter, maize seeds, and bags of fertilizer during the second week of February. In Korogwe District, the long, rainy season started in the first or second week of March. By that time, the maize field would have been plowed, planted, and fertilized. But it did not happen that way.

Whenever the tractor driver went to work in a village, he would report to the divisional secretary, the first person of contact in case of any problem. If the problem required my attention and action, the divisional secretary would report to me immediately. He was also responsible for handling any other administrative matters by collaborating with the ward secretary and the village leaders. In this incident, he didn't follow the normal protocol of implementation of rural development projects. When the tractor driver reported to him, he told him to first plow paddy rice fields belonging to Mombo Village and later go to Magamba Kwalukonge. He didn't ask me for a change in the plan; therefore, I was not aware of what was going on. He thought the work would be done in two days. He was wrong. The tractor broke down and needed major repairs. He could not dare to let me know about the problem because he knew he messed up big time. He was trying his best to get the tractor fixed, but the problem was that he could not get the parts needed. Meanwhile, the village leader at Magamba Kwalukonge was still waiting for the tractor. During the first week of March when the long rains began, the one hundred acres of maize field had not been plowed, and weeds began growing. By the end of March when the district director went to the village in preparation for president's visit, the weeds in the maize field were about ten inches high. He did not expect the farm would be like that because Magamba Kwalukonge was known for the good leadership in implementing development projects.

I did not say anything concerning the problem of the maize field on the way to Magamba Kwalukonge Village. I wanted the village leaders to tell the story, in their own words, about what happened. I did not want to be seen as if I were trying to defend myself. When we arrived at the village, the leader was in the office. Therefore, the conversation started right away. The District Development Director wanted to know why the field was full of weeds instead of maize plants. The village chairman pointed out that "The problem was caused by the divisional secretary who made changes in the plan without consulting with me or the village leaders. He retained the tractor to plow fields at Mombo Village, and when it broke down, he didn't inform anyone. But the District Agricultural Officer did everything according to the agreed plan. What happened was not his fault. We are completely satisfied with our collaboration with him. He is one of the best guys we ever had. You can ask anybody in the village, you don't have to take my word about him. He has helped us in so many different ways, including the planning and implantation of our development projects."

The District Development Director looked at me hoping that I would smile, but I kept a very serious face. He asked, "So what do we do now?" I said, "I will send another tractor tomorrow." And I told the divisional secretary, "Make sure this time the tractor comes straight to Magamba Kwalukonge." He smiled and said, "I am going to do that." The decision concerning the president's visit was to look for another village that would take the place of Magamba Kwa Lukonge. When our discussion was over, we passed by Mombo Town to drop the division secretary on our way to Korogwe. When I looked at the District Development Director, he appeared tense. I sensed that, for him, the problem was not over. I was almost sure he was going to try to show me who was the boss in Korogwe District.

The president's visit to three villages in Korogwe District went very well. Two months later, all heads of departments received a letter from the prime minister's office, directing a 20 percent reduction of workforce in terms of layoffs. In my case, it was very hard to perform that exercise because I was thinking about the families that would suffer as a result of layoffs. But it was a directive for all heads of departments to comply, and I did.

One weekend, I went to visit my elder brother, Gilbert Chilewa (fifth in the family ranking), in Tanga Town. At that time, he was a civil engineer with Tanzania Railways Corporation. We were at the Railways Corporation club at about 5:30 p.m. My brother was shooting darts when I heard a voice behind me say "Please, can I talk to you for a second." It was someone we knew each other very well. At that time, he was one of two personnel officers at the regional development director's office. He was very surprised to see me at that club because he knew I did not drink beer. After we stepped out of the clubhouse, he asked, "What are you doing here? I thought you don't drink beer?" I said, "I was not having a beer, I am just giving my brother company. I came to visit him and his family." He said, "I want to tell you something very confidential, please keep it to yourself." I told him "I will keep my word, I won't tell a soul."

Moving close to me, he continued in a very low voice, "The list of people laid off is complete and will soon be out, and for Korogwe District, your name was the first. Every committee member was surprised and thought something was not right with your District Development Director because they know you are a very good, competent, very intelligent, and hardworking person. Your name should not have been in the list. For your information, it has been removed. You have nothing to worry about." I looked at him and said, "I thank all the committee members for being fair and so considerate. And thank you very much for the information. I feel as if God sent me here to meet with you so that you can give me the good news."

As we were going back into the clubhouse, I asked him, "What about if I buy you one beer?" He declined the offer. He said, "No thanks, it is time I have to go home, but I would be happy to meet your brother." Inside the club, I introduced him to my brother and said jokingly, "Any day you see this guy in the club, give him beer and send me the bill." They talked for few minutes, and then he left. We left the clubhouse at 7:30 p.m. The following day I went back to Korogwe.

From the next day on, whenever I came in contact with the District Development Director, I would just smile. I would never say a word. Three weeks later, the list of laid-off workers came from the Regional Director's office. My name was not listed. Because the list was kept confidential, I decided not to show any sign that I knew what had happened. To everybody's surprise, a week later news went around that the District Development Director received a telegram indicating that another District Development Director was coming to take his place but didn't say where he would be transferred to. Rumors started to circulate that maybe he was laid off too. This went on for weeks, and people started to notice he was losing weight. Some said, "You see, what goes around comes around." He later received a letter for a transfer to Musoma Region.

CHAPTER 23

I Moved Back to My Home Region

Having dodged that bullet, I decided it was time to move back to Morogoro, my home region. I went and negotiated with one Agricultural Field Officer at the Regional Agricultural Office to switch work places with me. He was from Tanga Region; therefore, he eagerly agreed. By June 1997, I was back in Morogoro. This time, I was assigned to be the district coordinator for a maize development program. I was asked if I would be OK to work under a lady. I said, "Why not? I didn't mind at all." Therefore, in Morogoro, I worked under Mrs. Shayo, who was the District Agricultural Development Officer.

One day, I went to the Regional Agricultural Office to see Mr. Msumari at the Agricultural Publicity Office. As I was talking to Mr. Msumali, his co-worker walked in with a file in her hand. Mr. Msumali looked at me and said, "This is Maria Chale, she also works at this office." I tried my best not to show Mr. Msumali I was attracted to Maria. It was that kind of moment of love at first sight. Being a nice gentleman, I decided not to say anything to Maria. After all, she was busy at work. I thought if it was meant to be, I would get another chance to express my feelings about her. During the following two weeks, I met with Maria twice, but she did not like the idea of going for a date with me because she wanted first to know me well. Three months later we started dating.

One day, I saw a nice white SUV parked at her house. I was kind of jealous; therefore, the next day, I asked her who that person was. She said, "That was my uncle. He is the one who raised me. He came from Dar es Salaam, and he was here on official business. I have not had the time to tell you about him. He is the director of personnel at the national level in Dar es Salaam. Somehow, he knew about my relationship with you. In fact, he went to the Regional Personnel Office and asked for your confidential file. When he came to see me, he had all the information about you. He asked me if I loved you, and I said I did. But he was concerned that you may leave me. I told him I didn't think so because our relationship was very strong."

I assured Maria that nothing would come between us. However, I wanted to know why she didn't tell me that her uncle was the director of personnel, a very powerful position with direct influence on my job. I asked her, "What were you thinking? I could lose my job." She replied, "I never thought about that. By the way, have you heard the saying 'love is blind?'" I looked at her and said, "From now on, exercise your love with your eyes wide open. If you think this is over, you may be making a great mistake. We have to discuss how to convince him that our relation is serious. By the way, I don't know your tribal traditions. How can I meet with him?" She said, "It is kind of complicated. Let me do the talking first, and I will let you know the traditional procedure when the time is right." I said, "Oh boy, I didn't know I am getting into something completely different from our tradition. Just be very careful, keep me informed, and don't mess up." She assured me there was nothing to worry about.

Let me tell you about Maria at the time I met her. She had all the qualities I admired. She was beautiful, kind, sincere, intelligent, and hardworking. Apart from both of us being in the agricultural field, we had so many things in common. We both grew up in poor neighborhoods, and experienced a very tough childhood life. She grew up at Mpitimbi Village in Songea, southern part of Tanzania, and I grew up at Kilimatinde, in Dodoma Region, in the center of Tanzania and later moved to Kilosa Town in Morogoro Region. Even though we came from different tribes–she was Mngoni, I was Mkaguru–our attitude toward life and relationship with family members and other people was very similar. We both valued hard work and advancement in our careers. The thing I liked most, we were open to each other, and we spoke what was in our minds. This was what was missing in my life, someone who is not only a best friend but who plays an important role in shaping our life. I believed in the saying "two heads are better than one." I viewed Maria as my best friend and partner in life first, and as a wife second. And I let her know that. One late Saturday evening, as we set at the edge of a golf field, I said to her, "Let us talk about our relationship. Can you give me ten reasons why you love me and why we should get married? And I would do the same." We found out that our reasons were more similar than we thought. We were married July 26, 1978. In November 1, 1978, Winnie was born. My recollection of the reasons why she loved me when we met keeps my love toward her stronger.

In February of 1979, I was among thirty-five employees who took an exam arranged by the Ministry of Agriculture. The goal was to select the best candidates for a scholarship offered by the United States International Development Agency. It was the king of comprehensive exams, followed by an interview. Before the results came out, I was transferred to Kilosa, to be the District Agricultural Development Officer, a position held by a guy who retired. Therefore, in March of 1979, I moved to Kilosa Town.

I had been in this type of position for four years when I was at Korogwe District, Tanga Region. Therefore, I knew exactly what I was up to, busy days ahead, and long working hours. But it was the worst time to take over the responsibility of district development projects at the beginning of a long, rainy season. What I normally would like to do is to visit as many villages as possible for on-site assessment and discuss with local leaders about their problems and possible solutions. But I did not have time to do that for Kilosa District.

One of my first orders of business was to implement the rural mechanization program. This program was funded by the Rural

Development Fund to cover expenses for plowing village farms. I asked all tractor drivers to assemble in my office. I discussed with them all details about the project, their fieldwork allowance, and tractor service schedule. Then I asked them, "Who prepares your farms when you are out in the field far from home?" One of the drivers said, "My family, especially my wife, and I think it is the same for the other drivers too." I said, "I think it is quite unfair for you to go and plow other people's fields with a tractor while your wife prepares the family farm with a hand hoe. As long as I am your boss, this will not happen. From now on, make sure you plow your family farm first before you go to villages. Another thing, make sure you plant your crops using modern techniques because I want your farms to be a good example for your neighbors. If you need any kind of advice, I am here to help you. I wouldn't let my mother prepare her farm using a hand hoe either. I need a volunteer to go and plow her one-and-a-half-acre farm." One of the tractor drivers said, "Sir, this is the first time ever we get such a big help to prepare our farms. We thank you very much for thinking about us. I volunteer to go and plow your mother's farm. Just tell me where it is." When the meeting was over, all tractor drivers were motivated to go and perform their duty.

One day, I was on the way for my first one-week visit to twenty villages, when an officer on a motorbike came to a place we stopped for gas. He said there was an urgent message. I asked him if my family was OK. He said they were fine. Then he gave me a telegram mail from the Ministry of Agriculture. Before I opened to read it, I knew it was about the scholarship. I told the guy who gave me the letter, "Thank you very much for canceling my trip because this mail means the trip is over and maybe for good." He asked, "What do you mean?" I said, "I will let you know later." The information in the telegram was about the preparation I had to make for the scholarship. I was told to report at the Ministry Head Office immediately in Dar es Salaam for further instructions. To make the story short, I left in January 1980 for the bachelor of science program at North Carolina A&T State University, Greensboro, North Carolina, USA. My wife, Maria, joined me October of the same year.

CHAPTER 24

I Chose Not to Tell Anyone but a Close Friend

A total of six employees from the Ministry of Agriculture arrived at North Carolina Agricultural and Technical State University under the scholarship offered by the United States International Development Agency. Four of us were District Agricultural Development Officers, the other two were teachers from Agricultural Training Institutes, and one came from Sokoine University of Agriculture. Therefore, our course structure differed depending on our areas of specialty.

We arrived in January 1980. It was one of the coldest winter months in North Carolina. On the ground, there was about a foot of snow, and we did not have winter coats. We knew it was wintertime in North America, but we didn't expect that much snow. In fact, we were told that North Carolina winters were very mild. Therefore, the next day, the first order of business was to buy winter gear: boots, heavy socks, winter coats, gloves, and the type of hat that covered the head and ears. After I put on winter gear, being five feet and four inches tall, I looked like an Eskimo from Alaska. We didn't have a car; people looked at us as we struggled to walk on a foot of snow. It was quite a sight!

I wanted to bring my wife, but I didn't want the other guys to know because I was not sure how it was going to affect my plans. I chose not to tell even the guy whom I shared the two-bedroom apartment with. But there came a time that I had to tell one of the guys whom I trusted and who would not spill the beans. I was asked to produce a bank statement, and my account had very little money. Therefore, I asked Mr. Enock Mlingi to lend me three thousand dollars, which he did. In October of 1980, Maria joined me in Greensboro, North Carolina, and a few weeks later, we moved to our own apartment.

One Sunday morning, February of 1981, I walked to a nearby store to buy some groceries. It was very cold, and there was light snow on the ground. As I was going back home, holding bags of groceries on both hands, I stepped on black ice and fell like a big bag of potatoes. The groceries went flying in all directions. While my butt was still on frozen ground, I looked around to see if someone was watching me. When I didn't see anyone looking at me, I stood up and started to collect the groceries from the ground. This was a scene I would never forget. It was as if someone was telling me, "Welcome to the United States of America." When I told Maria what happened to me, she laughed her head off. But I didn't think it was funny at all.

During the spring semester of 1981, Professor M. R. Reddy of the Department of Crop Science advised me to enroll for a double major: BS plant science and BS agricultural education. I accepted his advice and enrolled. I took some classes during the summer. The goal was to complete my program at the end of 1981. I didn't tell the other guys that I was planning to enroll for masters during the spring of 1982. But I had a long discussion with Maria about how we would survive and also pay for my tuition. My USIDA scholarship was going to end as soon as I completed my BS degree. I asked Professor M. R. Reddy for a research assistant job in the soil chemistry lab so that I could pay my tuition. By fall of 1981, Maria was working two jobs, and I was taking classes and working in the lab. Our life was super busy, no weekends or holiday breaks.

Photo: Maria, at Greensboro North Carolina, USA,
August 1981.

December of 1981, we graduated in our BS programs, and the
other guys started shopping to prepare for a trip going home. When
they found out that Maria and I were not packing, they wanted to
know what was going on. I told them we were going to leave the
following month.

I did my thesis on "The Application of Municipal Sludge and the
Uptake of Heavy Metals by Soybeans, a Field Study." This study was
important for North Carolina because, during that time, there were
discussions about farmers applying municipal sludge on soybean
fields. But there was little information about whether the soybean
would be safe for animal and human consumption. The results of

this study indicated a high concentration of certain heavy metals especially lead, copper, and cadmium in leaves and pods. Some of these heavy metals were known to cause cancer. The conclusion was that sludge chemical analysis should be done to make sure it was safe for application on farmland.

I decided to do this study because it had practical applications in Tanzania. In Dar es Salaam, there were some residents who grew vegetables in various sites. When it rained, the water flooded the lower areas where, during dry weather, they were turned into farmland for vegetable production. These vegetables were sold at the local markets. My goal was to do an analysis to determine the safety of the floodwater, the soil, and vegetable plant material from various vegetable production sites in the city.

I graduated in May 1983 with a master's degree in agricultural education, with no debt. Maria and I went back to Tanzania and reported for duty at the Ministry of Agriculture. I was posted to Kigoma to take the position of assistant to the Regional Agricultural Development Officer. The following story is about my work life at Kigoma. It was quite an adventure.

CHAPTER 25

Do You Believe in Witchcraft?
I Don't and I Proved it

I never thought even in my wildest dreams that during my career with the Ministry of Agriculture, I would be sent to Kigoma Region, at the western border with Democratic Republic of Congo. During those days, Kigoma was known for three things: first, as a region very behind in development; second, as a region famous for witchcraft; and third, once you were sent to work in that region, it could be your home for a long, long time. I am going to tell you why I was sent to Kigoma.

When I reported for duty after completing my masters studies, I asked the director of Crop Production Department (name reserved) at the Ministry of Agriculture to give me a position in Mbeya Region. I wanted to go to Mbeya because it was one of the regions with a lot of agricultural activities due to good rainfall, fertile soils, and fantastic weather. My goal was to buy about thirty acres of prime land for the production of various types of fruits and vegetables.

Of course, I didn't tell the director about my plans. I came to find out he had a completely different idea. He wanted me to work in Dar es

Salaam for the crop monitoring project, which was being funded by the World Bank and the Tanzania government. In our discussion, I told him that I had a family, and housing was a big problem in Dar es Salaam, but Mbeya would be perfect for me. It was Friday, so he said, "Come to see me on Monday, I will have the decision." When I left his office, I went to ask one of his assistants to negotiate on my behalf. That was a very bad idea. I had no idea how their discussion went, but when I went to talk to him on Monday, his mood had changed completely.

As soon as I entered his office, he spoke to me with an angry tone. "I have decided to send you to Kigoma. You will be assistant to the Regional Agricultural Development Officer." I looked at him completely surprised and asked, "What happened? Why didn't you wait for me so we could talk about this before making such a decision? You know it is also about my family life too." He said that the decision was final. So that is how I moved to Kigoma.

Kigoma is a historic small town on the shores of Lake Tanganyika. At the time when I arrived, there was only one main street, going from the railway station to Mwanga, on the western side of the town. Having worked in larger towns before, I felt as if I was in a small village. My first impression was not good at all. I was thinking, "How am I going to live here?"

The Regional Agricultural Development Officer, Mr. Mtweve, was a very nice guy. I came to know later that his tribe was Mhehe, and he was from Iringa Region. Therefore, Mkaguru and Mhehe was a unique combination. Our level of education was the same; we both had master's degrees in agricultural education and extension. Since he had been in Kigoma Region for a long time, people started to circulate rumors that my arrival would make his request for transfer be granted. I just hoped that would not happen.

Whenever Mtweve was on official trip, I was in charge of the Regional Agricultural Office. The office was on the second floor of the Regional Administration Building. One time when he was on vacation, I had a discussion with the guy responsible for a maize seed production project. I asked him to prepare himself to go to the site within one week's time. The project was about fifteen miles away; therefore, I made sure he got everything he needed for the project.

When I didn't see him for two weeks I thought he had gone to the site. To my surprise, during the third week, one employee told me that he saw him at his house in Mwanga area. Therefore, I sent an urgent message asking him to come to the office. I wanted to know why he was still at home two weeks after he was given the project allowance. All I was looking for was a reasonable and sensible explanation.

The next day, the guy came to my office at about 8:30 a.m. Our conversation started by me asking him why he had not gone to the project site yet. He looked at me as if he wanted to say, "Who do you think you are to ask me such a question?" The guy was much older than me, and I had only been in the region for a few months. Therefore, to him, it seemed as if I was stepping on other people's toes. He said, "I have been sick, that is why I am still at home." I asked him, "Why you didn't report to me, or do you have a doctor's note?" He didn't answer. I told him, "The only reason I am not going to fire you is because I want to give you a second chance. Therefore, get ready because tomorrow morning at 10:00 a.m. I am going to send a driver to pick you up for the trip to the site. If you don't want to go, tell me right now so that I don't waste gas and driver's time." He gave me a long stare and then said, "OK, I will be ready." That look gave me an impression that he was up to something.

Two and half months later, I found, under my office chair where I put my feet, blood and a rat with the head hanging on the side. I held the tail using a napkin and threw it out of the office window. Then I asked the janitor to clean the bloodstain. I didn't tell him what happened, and I was glad he didn't ask. But I knew the old man I had a conversation with two weeks earlier was trying to scare me with witchcraft stuff. The problem was that I never believed in witchcraft, and I was sure his prank would not affect me. I did not tell anybody else, even my wife, about the incident. Because I knew she would be scared to death. The problem was that she was scared of that kind of stuff. And the worst part was that her friend, a co-worker (name reserved), was from Mwanga and was the same tribe as the old man. She too believed in witchcraft. Therefore, it would have been two against one, a battle I had no chance of winning. I just continued doing my normal duties.

About three months later, the old man came to my office looking very sick. I asked him, "You don't look so good. What is wrong? Are you OK" As he was sitting slowly on the office chair, he said, "Sir, I have been very sick for almost a week now. I need your help urgently." I asked him, "What is bothering you, have you been to the hospital for treatment?" He said in a low voice, "This is not something to be treated at the hospital. My ear hurts so much that I am not able to sleep at night. I have been told you are the only one who can help me." When I heard him say that, I knew he thought my body was protected from witchcraft such that what he did bounced back to him. Therefore, I decided to play that game. I stood up and looked directly at his eyes and asked, "Tell me one reason why I should help you after what you did to me? The problem is that you don't know where I come from and our traditions. For your information, I am coming from Kilosa, a place called Mtendeni at Kichangani. If you never heard about that place, go and ask anybody who knows. [I knew the name would scare him, but it was true; I came from Kichangani]. My parents knew I was coming to Kigoma, a place known for practicing witchcraft. Therefore, they made sure I was protected. I feel sorry for you. Give me two days to make my decision." He apologized and begged me to help him, almost in tears. He said, "Please help me because the pain is so unbearable, I can't sleep at night." I said, "OK, I will help you with one condition. Don't ever try this again to me or anybody else. You hear me?" He replied, "Me again, no, sir, I won't."

I started by saying, "Now, you listen to me real good. Tomorrow at exactly 10:00 a.m., go to the regional hospital and see Dr. Hemed. It is very important you are not late because it may not work. You don't have to explain to him about your problem. But follow all the instructions he will give you. If you won't do what I tell you, don't come back to me because it will be your fault." As he was leaving my office, he said, "Thank you very much, I will do exactly as you told me."

Dr. Hemed was the Regional Medical Officer. We knew each other when we were both in Morogoro Town. To me he was kind of a family doctor and a friend. I called him right away and said, "Tomorrow at ten in the morning, one of my employees is coming to see you for treatment of an ear infection. Please would you treat him with the best medicine because he is in so much pain such that he can't sleep at night. He said, "He is very lucky because I just received very good new medication." I said, "Thanks, Doctor, I know I can always count on you. I owe you a cold beer for that." He laughed. "Ha ha! It is OK."

Four days later, the old man entered my office, smiling. I asked, "Aha! What's the matter? You seem to be different compared to last Monday." He said, "I just came to thank you for helping me. For the last two days, I am able to sleep like a baby." I said, "I just hope you have learned something. Don't ever try to play tricks to someone you don't know very well. Now go back to work." He left smiling.

After having dealt with the problem successfully, I thought it was time to tell my wife about what happened to me. She said, "These are very dangerous people. Be very careful in the way you handle them. I heard so many frightening stories about Kigoma. I don't want to lose you, our kids need you." I said, "Don't you worry, I don't believe in that stuff. Therefore, I won't be affected. It is an old psychological trick. If you believe it, you develop fear, which would affect your immune system. As a result, you can get sick. The thing that I know for sure can kill you is when someone puts poison or a drug in your drink or food." She said, "Please just be careful, OK?"

In May 1985, I moved to Dar es Salaam City and joined the Extension Section of the National Coconut Development Program (NCDP). This program covered five coastal regions: Coast, Tanga, Lindi, Mtwara, and Morogoro. It was financed by the World Bank, West Germany, Britain, and the Tanzania government. We stayed at my father-in-law's house at Keko Magurumbasi.

During the summer of 1991, I joined North Carolina State University for a doctor of education program, focusing on agricultural education and extension. I didn't have a scholarship, so I went to school full-time and worked as student assistant part-time. My wife, Maria, worked with two jobs to help with tuition and family expenses. It was a very busy life because I had to help take care of Fred and Winnie by helping them with homework and preparing meals for them. I am proud to say they were very nice kids, performed well in school, and kept themselves out of trouble. My thesis was on "The Adoption of Integrated Pest Management Practices and Pesticide Use Among North Carolina Peanut Growers." Research committee members were the following: Professor Richard T. Liles, Professor Mike Linker, Professor John Pettitt, and the chairman was Professor David Mustian. I graduated in May 1998, debt free, thanks to Maria. During the following years, I worked at North Carolina State University, Murphy Farms, and Bland Landscaping Company.

CHAPTER 26

A Visit to My Roots

In June 2008, while on vacation in Tanzania after being away for nineteen years, I went with my brother Douglas Chilewa to Berega Village as part of a gold-exploration project. Berega is the village where our parents came from. In fact, there was a time when our late uncle Isac was chairman of Berega Village. Therefore, in a way, it was like going home. Colonial geological surveys indicated that there were gold deposits in certain areas of the mountains. We used a gold-detector equipment to look for signs of gold deposits at a number of sites, including riverbanks. Every site that showed a positive detection was marked for detailed exploration.

Photo: June 2008. I was explaining to the guy how the gold detector works.

Another village I visited for gold exploration was Idibo. The tribe in all the villages in this area were Wakaguru. I spoke very little Kikaguru, but everyone in the village spoke Kiswahili also, the national language. Their main activity was agriculture. The Idibo Village chairman took us to a farmer who made brown sugar out of sugarcane. On the way, we passed by the farmer's sugarcane field. It was in June, right at the beginning of the dry season, but the sugarcane plants looked excellent because the farm was in a floodplain area.

Photo: June 2008. At the side of the sugarcane field, the farmer grew tomatoes.

Idibo Village was in the western part of Morogoro Region, which received less rainfall compared to the eastern part. Therefore, after the end of long rains, some farmers grew crops like vegetables, maize, and sugarcane in the floodplain area. The next stop was at the farmer's house. Outside was a small group of ladies and kids in the process of making brown sugar.

Photo: June 2008. The lady is putting sugarcane pieces between two revolving poles. At the bottom there is an open container to collect the juice.

The type of the houses seen on the background and the environment was very similar to the house I grew up in at Kilimatinde in Dodoma Region. The whole process of making brown sugar was done manually. The next picture shows two women pushing a long poll that rotates the two poles in the center, producing crushing power.

Photo: June 2008. The two ladies would go round several times until all the sugarcane is done. The more pieces they have, the longer time it will take.

Photo: June 2008. In front of the two women is a group of children who gathered to observe what we were doing in the village. Their appearance is exactly the same as when I was their age.

Photo: June 2008. Farmer's wife and kids boiling the sugarcane fluid from the manual crusher.

After the crushing is done, they put the container on burning firewood. As the water evaporates, the material thickens. Then they pour it in a clean container to cool down and solidify. At that stage, it is brown sugar.

The village chairman informed us that businesspeople came from Dar es Salaam to purchase brown sugar from farmers. This would have been a good small business if they had a simple diesel-operated machine for making many pounds of brown sugar.

CHAPTER 27

The Roadside Open Farmers' Market

During the past nineteen years, when I was in the United States of America, so many changes took place. One of which was an increase in farmers' open markets on the side of the main road to Dodoma. Starting June, farmers bring to these open, roadside markets foodstuff such as sweet potatoes, tomatoes, beans, rice, sugarcane, and more. The unit of purchase is not by pound (or kilogram); the price is by a bucketful. My goal is to use part of the money obtained from the sale of this book to build a market shelter, toilet, and a coffee shop at the site I visited.

Photo: June 2008. I bought two buckets of beans (she put the beans in the yellow plastic bag), and she was trying to sell me more of her stuff. The price (June 2008) was 9,000 shillings per bucket, about 20 pounds. The exchange rate was 1,285 shillings per one dollar. Therefore, the price per bucket was about 7 dollars, or about 0.35 dollars per pound of beans. The advantage I had was that I had just changed my US dollars into shillings. Therefore, I felt the price was very cheap compared to how much I would pay for in the USA. The main reason was cheap labor. The other good thing was that the food materials were free of pesticides.

Photo: June 2008. Many buses stopped at these roadside
open farmers' market for passengers to buy some produce
at a very good price, compared to what they would pay
in the city.

I stopped at a small town called Gairo, a few miles along the
highway to Dodoma. There was a small group of farmers selling
their produce. A bicycle was a common method of transportation
in this area.

Photo: June 2008. A farmers' open market at Gairo. The white materials on the ground are shopping bags. They can hold as much as fifty pounds of produce.

Photo: June 2008. A farmer using an oxen cart for transporting various materials.

I found out that many farmers shipped their produce using oxen carts. This was a small improvement in farmer's way of life, compared to nineteen years ago when I left Tanzania to go to United States of America. At that time, the program of introducing the use of oxen for agricultural activities had just started.

CHAPTER 28

Putting into Practice What I Learned in Forty Years of Professional Life

Have you thought what would you be doing after you retire? What will be your physical and mental health? What kind of life will you have? Will you have enough money to live a comfortable life? If you haven't thought about that, take time to do so. Every birthday after fifty is a year closer to your retirement. That is a fact.

My decision to go into agricultural profession was based on what I wanted to do after I retired. When growing up, I participated in family farm activities, and I liked it. I got more interested in agricultural production and marketing after completing studies at Morogoro Agricultural College, now Sokoine Agricultural University. My goal was to learn as much as possible about modern farming so that I could have my own farm after retiring. Every position I held during my forty years of agricultural profession was part of my learning process. I have covered almost all areas of agriculture including horticultural projects, crop production and marketing, field research, animal production, landscaping, agricultural education and extension programs, personnel training and management, strategic project planning, implementation, and evaluation. In June 2008, I bought forty-seven acres, about twenty miles from Dar es Salaam, where I would put in practice what I have learned in forty years of my profession life. I would use this as a model farm for educating the local farmers free of charge and give part of the produce to orphanage. For forty years, I worked for institutions and made other people benefit from my hard work. After retiring, whatever I do is for me and my family and my cause.

In preparation for my life after retiring, I tried my best to maintain good health by eating healthy foods and vegetables. I drink only one glass of wine during dinner, I don't smoke, and I avoid stressful situations. I maintain a very good and loving relationship with my wife and kids, and I exercise regularly. As a result, I am in very good physical and mental health. The photo on the next page was taken June 2008 (signing papers), and the cover photo was taken in November 2011, at the age of sixty-six and nine months, eleven years after graduation. I think I look pretty good.

It was very important for me to know the long-term effect on my health of what I ate, did or didn't do. I decided to educate myself on the effects of smoking, alcohol, unhealthy foods, stress, vitamin and mineral deficiency, and bad relationships, gaining weight and the development of high blood pressure, being diabetic, having dementia, and other health problems. I knew that if I had these problems they would get worse and would be hard to manage as I grew older. I also learned that it is very important health-wise to keep my body and mind busy after retiring. That was one of the important reasons for having that farm.

At full operation, the farm will have irrigation facilities for all-year production of various types of vegetables, fruits, bananas, chicken, goats, and sows (female pigs). Solar panels and wind turbines will provide electric power for the farm. I want my readers to know that the purchase of this book is a contribution to two important causes: (1) building a market shelter, toilet, and coffee shop at the roadside market and (2) giving some of the produce free of charge to the HIV/AIDS orphanage.

Photo: June 2008. At the village, it was time for signing official papers for ownership of the farm. The man with the hat was the village chairman, the lady was the previous owner, and the others were witnesses.

This farm will provide much-needed casual-labor opportunities and training to the people living in the village. I will give intensive training on the process of running the farm to a family member who will serve as the manager. My responsibility will be supervision in making sure proper management is practiced and the vision of the project succeeds. This is going to be my time to pursue my passion, live my dream while helping others. Isn't that what life is all about?

CHAPTER 29

My Views About Life

It does not matter whether the new baby is Chinese, Indian, Mexican, Italian, Jewish, black, white, or brown. At the time it comes out into this world, it will cry. That action helps to open the lungs to start functioning. If the baby does not cry, whoever is helping with the delivery will make every effort for the baby to cry. Because crying is a sign the baby is alive. But to me, the crying can also mean an indication that in this world you have to struggle to survive.

At a very young age, children have no idea about life or where the money came from to buy food, clothes, or toys. They don't know why Mom or Dad, sometimes both, leave in the morning and come back in the evening or at night when they are already in bed. Some parents think that young children don't understand anything; therefore, they don't tell or involve them in discussion about what is going on in the family. That is a big mistake. The earlier the children understand the kind of life the family has, the better. If they know the financial situation and they are told that a trip to Disney World has to wait until the family economic situation improves, they will understand. Or if they are told why it is not possible to get a bicycle for Christmas this year, they will be happy to get another type of gift. Children should be told earlier on that each family is different because they have their own lifestyle. However, it is very important for parents to create and maintain a happy environment for the family, in all life situations.

What children are exposed to at home will have an impact on what they would become. If parents smoke, drink excessively, fight, or use a cursing language, when children grow up, they are likely to do the same. If parents don't care about checking on schoolwork or maintaining good behavior and being respectful, the children will act the same. There is a saying in Tanzania, "The way you raise the child will have an impact on what kind of a person he/she will become." Children need tough love by telling them what is right. A parent can be friendly to a child but should not give away the responsibility of parenting. My parents exercised the role of parenting very well, valued education and working hard, and insisted on the highest level of discipline and respect. As a result, every child was educated and later got a good job.

It is very important to let children know that life is never easy. At their age, going to school is a full-time job, and it means working very hard to get good grades. It means at certain times to switch off the TV or video games and study, do homework, or go to the library to rent a book. They should be told that their future would depend on how well they perform in school. They have to do well and pass the school exams; their parents won't do that for them. The problem is, when children are in elementary and middle school and sometimes even in high school, they think they will stay with their parents forever. Therefore, they don't work hard doing schoolwork because they know they will get from their parents whatever they need. Parents should tell children the facts about life, that when they reach adult age, people move out of family home and become independent. But before they move out, they need to have a job. The other fact is, each year millions of students graduate. Therefore, at the time of their graduation, there will be a very high competition for jobs. It is important to go into specialty areas such as engineering (e.g. mechanical, electrical, chemical, civil aviation), business management, computer science and technology, and other fields of science, where chances of getting a job are better.

The way I view life is this: everyone has to struggle to survive. Life becomes a little easier if we, as humans, recognize that we all have similar needs, and everyone is entitled to an equal opportunity to achieve them: good food, a house or place to sleep, clothing, love or being loved, respect, education, good job, medication when sick, living in a clean environment, and not being segregated against but being treated the same like any other person. If you are a manager or owner of a company, or are a businessman/woman, think about what is best for you, your employees and customers, and the company. Because you have the same needs and you need each other to survive. And if we all did our best to achieve that goal, the world would have been a happier place for all humanity. I hope my great-grandchildren will live in a better world.

There is a song that says, "It is not important what you take with you when you go but what you will leave behind." When you are a parent or grandparent, you have to think about the kind of life your wife/husband and children or grandchildren will be living when you leave this earth. As for me, I have done my part, and I know they will be OK. May God bless my family and all my readers.

Dr. Dudley Lameck, D.Ed

Photo: November 2011, Raleigh North Carolina, USA.
Thinking about life after retiring.

Edwards Brothers Malloy
Thorofare, NJ USA
April 9, 2012